RESEARCH PAPERS ON DEFENCE AND STRATEGIC STUDIES VOL. 1

STRATEGY, INDIA-CHINA AFFAIRS, AND CROSS-STRAIT RELATIONS

ANIRUDH PHADKE

Copyright © Anirudh Phadke
All Rights Reserved.

To my dear parents who were constant support of me

Contents

No one can defeat a powerful mind.

- Chanakya

Preface

After a lot of struggle back in late 2021 due to COVID-19 travel ban, I reached Singapore to continue my Master's degree at RSIS, NTU. During my academic journey, I learned and as well as gained a lot of experience regarding my subject matters. The degree was basically research intensive thus, I found myself writing a lot of research papers and other forms of academic reports.

All of my academic writings were highly graded and well received. Thus, idea of sharing it to other people, especially those interested/enrolled in my field came up in my mind. The end result is the book which you are going to read now. I thank my parents, family members, teachers in both undergraduate and post-graduate universities, friends, and well-wishers who were all constant supporters of my work. I also thank the guest contributor for adding more fruitful benefits to this book.

CHAPTER I

The Evolution of Strategic Thought

This subject is a fundamental and integral part for understanding defence & strategic studies. The subject matter carefully examines important ways of thinking about war and strategy, from the conceptual approaches articulated by its key strategists to the practical lessons across various domains. The subject deals with many theories regarding war & strategy, especially drawing attention to the historical, ideological, moral, social, political, cultural, economic, and technological, underpinnings that shaped their formulation and development. The subject provides readers with extensive opportunity to engage with major debates while evaluating the continuing validity of the theories pertaining to war and military strategies.

The subject apart from dealing with the nature, character and conduct of war across the span of human civilisation, it also studies various ways in which strategic theory helps its practitioners to determine the optimal use of military power in an increasingly complex environment. How can the military or government or any authority in power be effectively employed to fulfil the ends of policy?

Answering the above question and considering the vast subject matter of this topic, the following essays have been carefully crafted to present an idea of specific strategic decisions and grasp the intricacies of the strategy bridge that connects policy, strategy and other operations. The essays are also crafted in the following ways;

- It establishes the foundation of key strategic theories and their relevance in today's world.
- Employ insights from these theories to analyse and explain the conception and outcome of past wars and campaigns.
- The essays are of reading interest to general audience who want to improve or know more about defence & strategic studies.

• • •

Are any of Mahan's Principles of Sea Power Still Relevant in the 21ˢᵗ Century?

Image Credit: Yahoo News Singapore

Alfred Thayer Mahan (September 27, 1840 – December 1, 1914) was a United States Rear Admiral who was dubbed the "most significant American strategist of the nineteenth century" by John Keegan. Mahan's well-known book, 'The Influence of Sea Power Upon History, 1660-1783' and 'The Influence of Sea Power Upon the French Revolution and Empire, 1793-1812,' established him as the most important American author of the nineteenth century.

Mahan detected and propounded his sea doctrine aligning with the strategic position of the United States, as the nation reached the limits of its continental expansion by early the 1880s. He analysed the historical factors that formed the basis of British power. His sea doctrine stated that;

- The United States should be a world power.
- Control of seas is necessary for world power status.
- The way to maintain such control is via operating a powerful navy.

Mahan's theory of sea power still stands strong in the 21st century. Upon probing his book 'The Influence of Sea Power Upon History, 1793-1812' the following lines indeed prove the famous sea doctrine is still relevant in the 21st century.

"Notwithstanding all the familiar and unfamiliar dangers of the sea, both travel and traffic by water have always been easier and cheaper than by land."

The above statement conveys that Mahan travelled back into the history of mankind's struggle to develop his thesis concerning sea power. His sea power theory packed concisely states how different nations used/used the sea routes to achieve both military and non-military objectives. For example, Great Britain emerged as an undefeatable colonial power by establishing an advanced navy, thus controlling vast sea routes which resulted in the British becoming an economical super-power of the medieval and pre-modern eras. From a military perspective, Mahan gives an account of how Rome used the waters of the Mediterranean Sea to defeat Carthage. Thus, waters being a vital component of human evolution sea strategies stand deep-rooted till this day.

The above-quoted lines neglected the concept of the sky as this dimension was yet to be developed during the author's era. Considering the concept of the sky, even then air freight is 12-16 times more expensive than the same volume of sea freight cargo due to the volume of cargo a ship can carry at once as compared to an aircraft.

In Mahan's view, international commerce is essential for the success of America's economy, thus overseas military establishments are necessary to facilitate foreign trade and commerce. Mahan believed that commerce prospers by peace and suffers from war, so peace is the greater interest for great seafaring countries. To contextualise America's growing internal industrialism with a global role he emphasised the link between America's internal industrialisation and the ongoing economic transformation in China & India. There is a historical anomaly occurring in the Asian waters today that is the rise of two indigenous maritime powers concurrently with the United States' monopoly of the global commons.

As both the nations move up the economic and political hierarchy in the world, India and China have begun to attach new importance to maritime policy initiatives. Both the Chinese and Indian governments did not merely turn into their water boundaries but were adapting the expansive conceptions of maritime power pioneered by Mahan, who was also quoted as the evangelist of sea power. Paradoxically, like India and China, both embarked on similar emulation of Mahan they were also bound to run into each other's maritime aspirations.

It is not difficult to explain why both China and India are fascinated by Mahan's theories of Sea Power. Mahan's era was also the peak of the colonial period when all the major industrial powers began acquiring far-flung colonies and exploiting natural resources and markets. Thus, the shifting of supremacy began and turned towards Asian countries. This brief paper sheds light on Mahan's relevance of sea power doctrine in the 21st century by stressing the Chinese and Indian perspective and connecting it with Mahan's identification of four main components of sea power- seaborne commerce, merchant shipping, navy, and overseas bases.

The first pillar of sea power according to Mahan is robust domestic industrial production and its export to overseas markets. This led to the further derivative statement that disrupting a rival's sea-borne trade would be at the heart of modern warfare. Therefore, the construction of modern navies that could achieve this objective in decisive battles at sea. If protecting the sea lines of communication between the centres of industrial production is the goal, then the third derivative statement would define itself. It was necessary to have naval bases and facilities to protect the navies from their competitors. Mahan asserted that merchant ships and naval ships in nations without overseas facilities were like "land birds unable to fly far from their shores."

With the advent of the 21st century, all three components of sea power have been united for India and China, and Mahan has become an inspiration for leaders in both countries. The Maritime Military Strategy published by the Ministry of Defence, Government of India, draws a connection between "economic prosperity and increasing naval capabilities, which will attract investments, enable the nation's natural resource development, and ensure the nation's maritime interests are respected". China has become acutely aware of the profound relationship between national economic development and strategic sea power under Xi Jinping's leadership and has constantly affirmed the determination to build a strong navy capable of fighting wars with modern technology. Both the nations have an equal share of maritime disputes, and the need to protect a large water body of Exclusive Economic Zone (EEZ), Andaman & Nicobar Islands and Lakshadweep has been an important motivation behind India's naval modernisation. The latter theme can be found behind the Chinese plans for navy advancements.

Thus, the sea-borne commerce component will be in the disguise of 'resource security' between India & China. As both the nations have been the most populated countries in the world, food imports, and all other major consumer goods will be incoming into these nations via Asian waters. The massive dependence on imports will put the two Asian giants in an aggressive race to set their respective strong foothold for the Indian Ocean Region in upcoming years.

Mahan also stresses establishing colonies as a vital component of sea power doctrine. In today's context, this element can be interpreted as naval bases and overseas merchant logistical establishments. In a world of growing industrial production and worldwide commerce, Mahan saw the link between a nation and its trading system with its colonies as vital. The worldviews of the Chinese and Indian leaders as they led their respective countries into a fresh engagement with the rest of the world could not have been more unlike than Mahan's. Both territories were part of naval powers such as the United Kingdom, and their governments regarded foreign outposts as the exact emblem of colonialism and its enhanced form of imperialism.

Both Indian and Chinese administrations remained naturally hostile to the big powers' forward military presence, which grew considerably with the intensity and globalisation of the Soviet-American competition during the Cold War. As fast-growing emerging countries, India and China became the most vociferous opponents of foreign bases, citing both lofty ideological principles and immediate national security worries about big powers intruding in their affairs. The setting, however, has radically changed in the early twenty-first century.

As both these developing nations underline the importance of maritime purpose, resource security, and their larger global political responsibilities, both China and India are signalling the political will to deploy their navies far from their domestic waters. This in turn bound to result in a more intensive consideration of forwarding military presence abroad.

If China's interest in establishing a forward military presence in Myanmar was viewed as a one-of-a-kind strategic decision, its efforts to purchase naval bases around the Indian Ocean have gotten increasingly aggressive in recent years. China's 'String of Pearls' idea in the Indian Ocean depicts the communist giant's building of marine infrastructure in South Asia, allowing the dragon to link to the Western world through Gwadar in Pakistan and beyond the South China Sea in the East.

Currently, India is looking at chances to acquire infrastructure that would allow it to operate outside of its seas. Now, India operates airbases at Farkhor, Tajikistan, and Hambantota in Sri Lanka. The nation holds merchant logistical bases at Muscat (in Oman), Chabahar port (in Iran), and Madagascar. Further, the country has naval bases at North Agalega Island (in Mauritius) and Seychelles. In the year 2017 India signed a naval cooperation agreement with Singapore.

Meanwhile, China under the administration of Xi-Jinping has its fully operational military (naval) and logistical base at Djibouti which is famously dubbed the 'horn of Africa.' China has attempted to negotiate an agreement to build a naval station in Tanzania, farther south, and now in the Atlantic around the Cape of Good Hope. If these pacts become fully operational, then China would establish an unbreakable Atlantic gateway which could result in leading the dragon close to the American-dominated Mid-Atlantic region.

India and China's forward military presence policies arise from their navies evolving from forces designed for coastal protection and denying hostile countries access to their neighbouring seas to instruments capable of projecting force well beyond their borders. The fact to be noted is the security challenges of the world in the early twenty-first century that is rooted in the Asian region identified by Mahan. Mahan's Sea doctrine theory when implemented to probe the forward military presence of the United States, India, or even China shows a clear picture of the current race to dominate Indian Ocean Region.

Whether or if India and China eventually acquire military sites, their new outward marine orientation represents a fundamental structural shift in their worldview. Both the tiger and the dragon see a link between rising to great power status and establishing a strong naval capability.

Because of Mahan's preoccupation with sea power, his successors coined the geopolitical framework of 'Eurasia,' as well as the apparent battle between 'sea power' and 'land power.' Halford Mackinder viewed the competition as involving Russia, the rest of Europe, and Central Asia. Whoever controlled the pivot area, Mackinder concluded, would dominate Asia. In the first decade of the twenty-first century, the collaboration between the People's Republic of China (PRC) and Russia to reclaim its influence over Asia through promoting the Shanghai Cooperation Organisation (SCO) has also added to the general importance of the notion of Eurasia. But the notion of Eurasia's centrality in our present geopolitical understanding of the world may not necessarily survive the rise of China and India and their growing maritime abilities.

Alfred Mahan made the foresighted comment that whoever controls the Indian Ocean controls Asia, and this body of water is the gateway to the seven seas. He also stated that the fate of the planet would be decided on its waterways in the twenty-first century. This appears to be the case since the Indian Ocean plays a role in forming the current world order. In the current geopolitical environment of Asia, India will be more reliant on water bodies for survival, growth and development.

Mahan predicted China's great potential and suggested that the United States would have to be cautious about the emergence of Asian communists. In a letter to the editor of the New York Times in 1893, Mahan advocated for the annexation of Hawaii by the United States as a vital first step in gaining control of the North Pacific. 'The enormous majority of China.... may fall to one of those drives which have in the past buried civilisation under a wave of barbarian invasion,' Mahan warned if the US did not act.

While the People's Republic of China has developed new international relationships, it has also been modernising its military, with a special focus on naval modernisation. On the other hand, only two forces are challenging India's drive towards increasing its military presence in its backyard (Indian Ocean)- the United States' current dominant maritime presence and China's growing might Following the 9/11 tragedy, India-US ties have grown stronger, partly as a result of perceived Islamist Jihadist dangers in the area, but also as a result of China's rising prominence. In 2005, the US State Department stated that "the objective of the United States is to assist India in becoming a significant international power in the twenty-first century." We are completely aware of the ramifications of that remark, including military repercussions.

However, China, on the other hand, is expected to be a tough competitor for India. This is the new big game that might take place in the Indian Ocean, with the entire globe watching. As far as the PLAN is concerned from a geostrategic perspective, the US is the PRC's greatest threat and is attempting to encircle China. Thus, the PLAN considers naval modernisation as a critical component of its defence in any near-term future conflicts. We can expect China to engage in a permanent naval presence in IOR soon. There could be stiff maritime competition between China and India as per all the pillars of sea doctrine stated by Alfred Thayer Mahan.

Chinese involvement in the IOR is evidence of a revisionist state seeking to undercut US policy; similarly, China's encirclement of India is seen on many fronts. In other words, China will continue to rapidly expand its presence and exert ever-greater influence in the IOR, while India, under the Modi regime, will evolve its policy-strategy calculus and forge ahead to remain dominant as well as relevant as a net security provider, with the US pursuing the role of a mediator.

Thus, with the brief answer to the question, we can conclude that Alfred Thayer Mahan's Sea doctrine still holds strong relevance in the 21st Century. Still, today, fighting a foreign war remains a product of command of the sea. The means of warfare may have changed but the core objectives remain the same. Simply looking at the world map, our planet is covered with 71% water. It means that water bodies as a means of sea-borne commerce and battle arena never get out of fashion atleast till mankind's existance.

References & Endnotes

1. MAHAN'S CONCEPTS OF SEA POWER. (n.d.). Retrieved from https://www.jstor.org/stable/45236517

2. The Influence of Sea Power on History | AHA. (n.d.). Retrieved from https://www.historians.org/teaching-and-learning/teaching-resources-for-historians/teaching-and-learning-in-the-digital-age/imperialism-european-american-and-japanese/what-is-imperialism/the-influence-of-sea-power-on-history

3. Barrios, Katherine. "A Debate on Air Freight versus Sea Freight: Which Should You Choose?" Xeneta.com, 2018, www.xeneta.com/blog/air-freight-versus-sea-freight.

4. MARITIME STRATEGY of INDIA and CHINA: INFLUENCE of ALFRED THAYER MAHAN. www.indiannavy.nic.in/sites/default/themes/indiannavy/images/pdf/resources/article_7.pdf. Accessed 17 Oct. 2022.

5. Nus.edu.sg, 2022, www.isas.nus.edu.sg/wp-.

6. (PDF) Maritime Power: India and China turn to Mahan 1 | C .... (n.d.). Retrieved from https://www.academia.edu/37262357/Maritime_Power_India_and_China_turn_to_Mahan_1

7. "China Is Trying to Build an Atlantic Naval Base." Popular Mechanics, 11 May 2021, www.popularmechanics.com/military/a36385283/china-

trying-to-build-atlantic-naval-base/.

8. "Digitale Bibliothek Erkenntnisse Finden Und Austauschen." Dokumen.pub, dokumen.pub/samudra-manthan-sino-indian-rivalry-in-the-indo-pacific-. Accessed 17 Oct. 2022.

9. The Geopolitical Vision of Alfred Thayer Mahan – The Diplomat. (n.d.). Retrieved from https://thediplomat.com/2014/12/the-geopolitical-vision-of-alfred-thayer-mahan/

10. Background Briefing by Administration Officials on U.S .... (n.d.). Retrieved from https://2001-2009.state.gov/r/pa/prs/ps/2005/43853.htm

• • •

(The following article is a different kind of attempt to deliver the content. It is written in a letter format rather than traditional research paper)

Finding Modern Day Relevance in 'The Art of War'

Dear Master Sun (Sun Tzu),

My warm greetings to you general. I am a young, vibrant, and energetic student of strategic studies. **My keen interest in the military and politics landed me in the weird world of strategy, politics, international relations, and war.** Looking into my background experience, I have no military experience nor strategic desk work training. I am still at a budding stage and have read your critically acclaimed literature 'The Art of War' during my learning phase in undergraduate studies. Finally, I got a chance to write to my favourite military strategist/thinker as a part of my coursework assignment on the subject called 'The Evolution of Strategic Thought' from S. Rajaratnam School of International Studies (RSIS), Singapore.

In that context, I am writing this letter from a student perspective reviewing some of your critical opinions and thoughts from the book 'The Art of War.' The world embarked on a journey filled with wars and saw the changing dynamics of war from being mere land & naval warfare and now producing weapons of mass destruction and cyber (virtual) warfare. Keeping in mind this latter statement, I will also jolt down some of my very own thoughts on how your work is practically implemented in today's world.

Firstly, I would like to share the good news that your timely classic 'The Art of War' has survived through many centuries and has been considered one of the greatest military science pieces of literature of all time by famous French revolutionary and world war figures such as Napoleon, Mao Zedong, Fidel Castro, General MacArthur, and Joseph Stalin. Your ideologies now represent contemporary behaviours and geopolitical happenings of the Chinese government and its military wing- The People's Liberation Army (PLA).

Your book 'The Art of War' divided into thirteen chapters written in form of quotes and points mesmerise me and I agree with the values it presents. One such famous quote from your book 'know your enemy and know yourself and fight a hundred battles without danger' and the other 'know yourself but not your enemy and win the battle but lose another' still stands fresh as written in your times. We need to be always careful of enemies and prepare ourselves for different kinds of responses enemies have, thus, not just likely to focus on the central part of planning. I could like to touch upon six key points from your work.

The first aspect which you touched upon was how one must understand the **significance of terrain**. One must know key features of terrain such as urban areas, deserts, valleys, rivers, hills, and mountains as these features dictate how to gain a strategic advantage over any battle. In 2020 India and China engaged in fierce hand-to-hand combat near the Line of Actual Control (LAC) in Ladakh. Although India had a victory followed by huge losses of its soldiers, both nations struggle to solve the problem because their administrations fail to understand the concept of terrain and separation of boundaries. Right from the beginning, no roundtable discussions were able to identify who owns which part of the key areas of terrain along the Indo-China border stretching all over the Himalayas.

Secondly, your quote 'If you know the enemy and know yourself, you need not fear the result of a hundred battles. If you know yourself but not the enemy, for every victory gained you will also suffer a defeat. If you know neither the enemy nor yourself, you will succumb in every battle rightly can be phrased as **Information is key to success**. In today's scenario, every piece of information is digitalised and stored in form of data and nations devise strong cyber defence capabilities to guard themselves against data thieves called hackers. Thus, countries move up the ladder to success by processing relevant geopolitical happenings form of gathering information.

The next quote which I would like to place here is "There is no instance of a nation benefiting from prolonged warfare." This aptly suits the **US withdrawal from Afghanistan**. The long insurgency of nineteen years by the US did not reap edible fruit and finally resulted in handing over the US' backed administration to the Taliban. Currently, the territory under the Taliban called as 'Islamic Emirate of Afghanistan' created much further rising tensions among local communities.

Fourth, you mention the use of spies and assassins in your strategy guide. In today's scenario, the core concept remains the same while the execution of this item has much evolved then it was during your times. Today many countries established special cell units called **intelligence departments**, whose sole work is to collect and analyse the movement of enemies. Furthermore, the military has a specialised branch of well-trained men usually labelled as **special forces**.

For example, India has special units under each of its military divisions called Para SF (for the army), Garud Command Force (for air force), and MARCOS (for navy). These units deal with the functions of spies and assassins belonging to your era. Raised in July 1966 the **9th Para SF** (also called ghost operators) of the Indian Army due to its highly secretive nature are trained to conduct secret operations like intelligence collection deep into foreign soil and go depths of 7 to 50 kilometres into enemy territories. They are also well-trained assassins to take out high-profile enemy targets in a hostile region of Jammu and Kashmir. The unit operates independently thus making them perfect silent assassins in the modern era.

Since you have told us, good intelligence is needed for **deception**, I am bringing the latter term as the fifth key point of this letter. For example, the US the world's most powerful military increases its portion of its defence budget each year to meet the 21st century scientific standards on tactical camouflage, concealment, and deception. William Casebeer who is a research area manager for human systems at Lockheed Martin's Advanced Technology Laboratories laid a tendinous emphasis on the importance of shaping enemy perception to breed success either by winning the battle or even a better option as stated by you master sun that is obviating warfare.

Further, as a DARPA (Defense Advanced Research Projects Agency) host, William like every other prominent military theorist suggests that creating illusions helps soldiers egress from war zones safely back to their base. The best example can be found in World War 2. The allied powers built massive inflatable army dummies including tanks which proved tactical to ground troops. This strategy vastly affected the key decisions of Nazis at various stages of war leading to their downfall. The British invited Jasper Maskelyne, a renowned magician to lead their deception development team called 'Magic Gang'. They successfully spoofed German field marshal Erwin Rommel by disguising 1000 tanks in the north as common trucks while leading an attack from the south with 2000 decoy tanks. Today the military tanks and decoys are highly realistic due to modern technology and can go unrecognised within a few hundred feet.

Another tool used by law enforcement agencies in modern days is 'flash bangs' (otherwise called stun grenade) is considered a handy deception tool. Its loud noise of 170 decibels and intense flashing of light shuts down the human sensory system for a few minutes.

Followed by deception, the changing dynamics of warfare bring the concept of irregular wars. Master Sun, you mention **strange tactics** in your guide 'The Art of War' which had limited scope during your times. Today many countries combine the potential action of regular and irregular warfare techniques by mending unorthodox war strategies, otherwise called as unethical means of war. I can understand Master Sun as you quote this line in your work "If you are good at irregular warfare, you will be as inexhaustible as the sky and the earth."

General David Petraeus during his days in Afghanistan learned to mend your works by applying them to real-life war scenarios. During one point of time off the surge in Afghanistan, he directed the attachment of two common infantry battalions with that of the Joint Special Operation Task Force. Thus, the augmentation of two different units enabled him to gain control over twice the size of locations which he had as an outcome of his previous plan.

Briefly, I am happy to conclude that your works are much appreciated even in the 21st century and I hope the same will be carried beyond. The strategy by no means exhausts from this world since it is the core of all planning systems. So, the dynamics of war may keep on changing but not the strategy. Thus, Master Sun, your work is considered evergreen literature for military thinkers and even **business managers**. Evan Spiegel, CEO (Chief Executive Officer) of Snapchat felt threatened by Facebook's aggressive advancements into its market domain. So, he handed over a copy of your book to each of his employees to have them formulate a new strategy to overcome ruthless competition.

I realise that you may not be able to reply easily, so do not feel obligated to do so.

Yours Sincerely,

Anirudh Phadke

References & Endnotes

1. Comparative Study of Sun Tzu and Kautilya on Military Affairs; by Shantanu K. Bansal | C3S India | Chennai Centre for China Studies. www.c3sindia.org/archives/comparative-study-of-sun-tzu-and-kautilya-on-military-affairs-by-shantanu-k-bansal/.
2. Student paper submitted to Georgetown University.
3. "A Quote from the Art of War." Www.goodreads.com, www.goodreads.com/quotes/17976-if-you-know-the-enemy-and-know-yourself-you-need.
4. 9 PARA SF - Ghost Operators of the Indian Army | Para Commandos. www.youtube.com/watch?v=e8YbJDTEfZI. Accessed 17 Oct. 2022.
5. Macknik, Stephen L., and Susana Martinez-Conde. "Battlefield Deceptions." Scientific American Mind, vol. 28, no. 2, Feb. 2017, pp. 18–19, https://doi.org/10.1038/scientificamericanmind0317-18.
6. Gen David Petraeus. "'The Art of War': As Relevant Now as When It Was Written." The Irish Times, The Irish Times, 26 Mar. 2018, www.irishtimes.com/culture/books/the-art-of-war-as-relevant-now-as-when-it-was-written-1.3440724.
7. Moss, Caroline. "After Meeting Mark Zuckerberg, Snapchat's CEO Immediately Bought Every Employee a Copy of 'the Art of War.'" Business Insider, businessinsider.com/spiegel-gave-employees-the-art-of-war-2014-1. Accessed 17 Oct. 2022.

CHAPTER II

The Analysis of Defence and Security Policy

This subject under defence and strategic studies deals with concepts of defence/security policies. Generally, a careful study of defence policies can reveal deep-seated, often unstated assumptions that are grounded in a number of key academic concepts that will be examined in the essays under this chapter.

The following subject matter tries to address the questions pertaining to national security policies of a country. For example;

- How and why policymakers identify and prioritise what national interests must be secured and defended;
- How policymakers can approach the problem of how to secure and defend national interests; and
- What kinds of potential problems can these measures designed to secure and defend national interests create that can undermine the entire national security edifice.

While the above questions are vast in nature, my essays in this subject matter will address one such issue pertaining to national security and will attempt to address one of the questions above.

The following titles can be used by general audience and other strategic thinkers for deep understanding of this subject matter.

- Barry Buzan, An Introduction to Strategic Studies: Military Technology and International Relations (Houndmills: Palgrave Macmillan, 1987).
- Stuart E Johnson, Martin C Libicki and Gregory F Treverton (eds.), New Challenges and New Tools for Defense Decisionmaking (Santa Monica: RAND, 2003).
- Colin S. Gray, Strategy and Defence Planning: Meeting the Challenge of Uncertainty (Oxford: Oxford University Press, 2014).

• • •

ANIRUDH PHADKE

The Viability of Deterrence Strategies in the 21ˢᵗ Century

Abstract

In the 21ˢᵗ century, the world saw a major shift in deterrence strategies such as from nuclear to cyber to economic sanctions. This paper is an attempt to bring out the viability of deterrence by analysing the current geopolitical happenings around the world. Further, this paper brings out how non-nuclear states have developed a reliable deterrence doctrine despite lacking nuclear power. The key takeaways are;

- *The deterrence strategies are still viable in the 21ˢᵗ century.*
- *Cyber Deterrence is still in its infant period. Countries are adopting more reliable forms of deterrence such as economic sanctions.*
- *Sir Churchill's proclamation still holds. By the end of the day, nations prefer the military as a means of deterrence to achieve their goals. Thus, military deterrence stands for God forever. That is why the slogan of an army is always apt- Always Ready, Always here.*
- *The nation's goal is to protect its sovereignty at any cost. Thus, it leads them to bump into other nations in form of war at some given point in time. So, the most reliable instrument for protection is deterrence.*

Bernard Brodie, a famous military strategist and father of deterrence theory wrote Strategy in the Missile Age (1959), in which he outlined the framework of the deterrence theory. Brodie concluded that deterrence by second-strike capability would lead to a more secure outcome for both parties. He stated the hardening of land-based missile locations was important for the second-strike capability force to have first-strike capabilities to provide the stasis necessary for deterrence.

Sir Lawrence Freedman, the notable deterrence researcher who pinned his viewpoint on deterrence theories, said that it works best when clear red lines exist when vital interests are at stake, and when capabilities are known by the host. In a simpler perspective, deterrence denotes 'the action of discouraging an action or event through instilling doubt or fear of the consequences. For example, the latter statement when put into practical terms as 'nuclear missiles remains the main deterrence against possible aggression.'

The popularity of deterrence theory saw immense growth during the Cold War periods. During this hostile state of high global tensions, a deterrence strategy was aimed at preventing aggression by the hostile communist power centres- the USSR and its allies, communist China, and North Korea. In particular, the strategy was devised to prevent a nuclear attack by the USSR or China.

In the 21st century, notable military strategies from all over the world have delivered how deterrence plays a vital role in the current global order. The concept of deterrence has changed how nations convert political tensions into war and prevent the same from happening.

RAND Corporation analyst Karl Muller analyses different approaches to conventional deterrence, arguing that it will remain a major tool for the prevention of war. He strongly disagreed with those scholars who argued nuclear weapons have superseded conventional deterrence. Since the threat of nuclear weapons was not justifiable with the current global order, investments in conventional deterrence remained the topmost priority. Alexey Arbatov affiliated with the Institute of World Economy and International Relations in Moscow dwells upon the self-destructive tendencies inherent with nuclear deterrence. The nuclear nations involve in a continuous quest for new weapon systems such as hypersonic missiles, weapons of mass destruction (MAD), and integration of new modifications in existing stockpiles which could erode strategic stability.

The best example of how nuclear deterrence holds its viability still today can be found in the geopolitical happenings of North Korea and the United States. Both nations frequently create high tensions of possible nuclear conflicts. Communist Korea has always been stricken with poverty and a lack of sufficient survivable resources. Each time when the nation gets depleted of resources, North Korea tests and fires its new weapon systems. This in turn raises huge security concerns for the US military stationed in Camp Humphreys, Pyeongtaek in South Korea. Thus, to nullify the effects and push North Korea towards a controlled arms production environment, the United States shook hands with North Korea by providing sufficient food aid worth $800 million.

The United States proved to be the largest essential resource exporter to North Korea since the times when both nations acted hostile to each other. Thus, North Korean leaders channelised their funds towards a sole source that is to produce nuclear missiles and force the democratic power to lend resources that the nation did not possess. Although North Korea shut down its nuclear reactors in exchange for food aid from the United States, nuclear deterrence indeed proved viable here to achieve the objectives.

Another example of nuclear deterrence can be found in the recent geopolitical happenings of China and Japan in their Taiwan card. Mid this year, The Chinese Communist Party (CCP) aired a video in which it warned Japan of a full-scale war including a nuclear response if the island nation interferes with China's treatment of Taiwan. The communist giant under the administration of Xi-Jinping singles out Japan as the one exception to China's policy to not use nuclear-propelled weapons against non-nuclear powers.

The video aired on the Chinese media sharing platform 'Xigua' quoted that China will use nuclear bombs first and continuously until Japan withdraw its intervention in Taiwan. Further, the video showed the Chinese intentions to use nuclear weapons against Japan, till the nation declares unconditional surrender for the second time. Although the video was deleted from Xigua, additional copies were uploaded to YouTube and Twitter. These nuclear threats were delivered as the result of Japanese officials recognising Taiwan's sovereignty. Japan must give diplomatic immunity to Taiwan for securing the upper hand in the East China Sea dispute.

Japan ceded its aggressive advancements in the Taiwan card as soon as the communist giant declared a call for nuclear strikes against the nation. If this major incident happens, it will be a highly threatening situation for both Japan and Taiwan. If that is the case, Japan and the United States must defend Taiwan together. Meanwhile, the Chinese Ministry of Foreign Affairs spokesperson Zhao Lijian urged Japan to adjust its mentality over Taiwan's issue. Further, he conveyed that Japan must show respect for China's sovereignty over Taiwan which is crucial for upholding regional peace and stability among the sinicized countries.

Another evolving example of nuclear deterrence can be evidenced between the two Asian powers- China, and India. Both the nations possess strong nuclear capabilities and deeply developed nuclear doctrines. While many analysts argue the nuclear deterrence failure of India against China in the backdrop of Ladakh skirmishes in 2020, it should be noted that due to much evolved nuclear technologies and doctrines between the two Asian powers, the recent Ladakh standoff subdued without any major conflict including a call for nuclear strikes Both India and China pursue defensive nuclear strategies and bureaucrats not only understand the importance of avoiding nuclear conflicts but also retain complete authority over the nuclear command control. Both the nations have remained optimistic that nuclear weapons are a stabilising factor in their bilateral relationship rather than a source of concern- even though the tempering effects of economic interdependence may be a warning and the strength of both the countries' nuclear no-first-use policies is facing growing internal scrutiny.

Despite the potential for future instability and constant high political tensions between the two nations, there is a chance of holding an official bilateral nuclear dialogue between Modi and Xi-Jinping soon as there is much support for expert-level engagement to discuss mutual concerns.

Although if the bilateral nuclear dialogue occurs, it does not necessarily mean that China and India will turn into friends from enemies, for sure any future conflicts that occur between these two nations does not turn into a nuclear conflict since nuclear technologies keep rapidly evolving in both India as well as China. Thus, this example is incredibly unique in nature being a solution where both nations benefits. Thus, nuclear deterrence holds viable for China and India to escalate their political tensions into a full-scale war.

Nuclear deterrence in the 21st century is very much hyped. The public floats on the notion that nuclear states enjoy a superior position to non-nuclear states. This is not the case for every state. Even before the start of this century, when the United States rested as one of the major nuclear superpowers failed to cripple the smaller non-nuclear state- Cuba. Even today Cuba does not possess nuclear, chemical, biological, or even long-range ballistic missiles. The nation is an active participant in many of the major non-proliferation treaties and regimes. The non-nuclear nations have also developed strong warfare capabilities and proved that a nation certainly does not need nuclear weapons to go against nuclear nations.

The non-nuclear nations' main concern for developing deterrence which does not involve nuclear weapons is because it delivers the threat of total annihilation. So, if the enemy territory used nuclear weapons as pinned down in the second-strike capability doctrine, the smaller non-nuclear states stand no chance of survival. Thus, non-nuclear states, especially smaller countries found their best interests in developing some form of conventional deterrence as war could prove catastrophic. Furthermore, the non-nuclear states have found that when employing deterrence strategies should take not not to escalate diplomatic tensions or inadvertently highlight their weakness in process.

"Then it may well be that we shall by a process of sublime irony have reached a stage in this story where safety will be the sturdy child of terror, and survival the twin brother of annihilation."- Sir Winston Churchill.

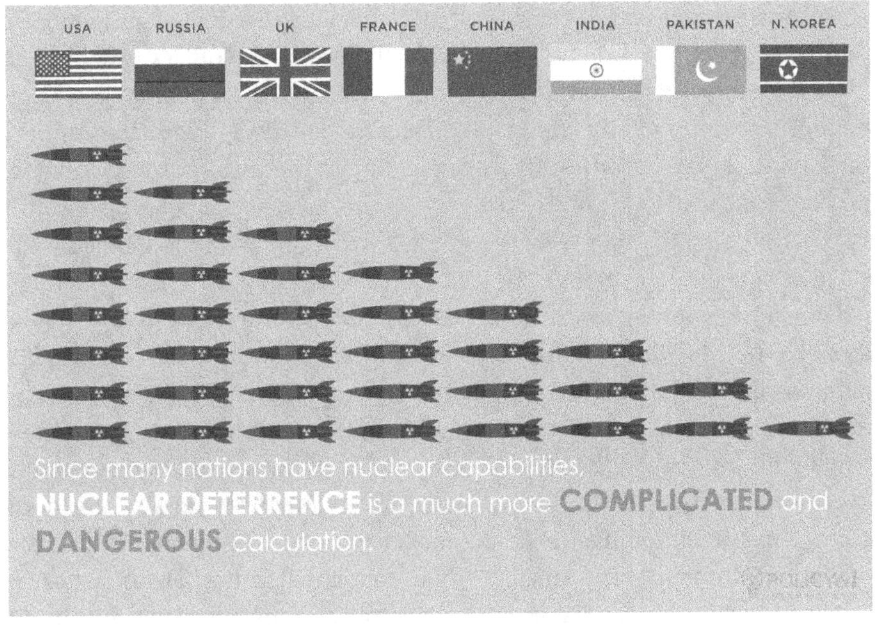

Image Credit: POLICYed

The above indeed proves that the fear of destructive nuclear retaliation will paradoxically create a stable strategic environment where nuclear-powered states are deterred from using nuclear weapons against one another. Sir Churchill's proclamation was proven right in this regard; the Cold war ended without direct military conflict between the two competing nuclear powers- the US and the USSR. Further, the total destructive component of nuclear weapons paved way for emerging new security dynamics of the Cold War era. Especially the smaller and politically weaker nations sought the help of security analysts to develop a conventional deterrence doctrine which can be pursued by them eventually. The non-nuclear states developed their doctrine from traditional deterrence strategies such as 'deterrence by punishment' and 'deterrence by denial' by opting out of nuclear components.

Most nation's not possessing nuclear weapons followed a common pattern in executing deterrence strategies. For example, Singapore being a smaller nation enjoyed an elevated level of national security by implementing deterrence along with diplomacy which is known as the 'twin Ds.' It was not feasible for a state, especially a smaller one to just stick to one aspect of twin Ds. Thus, deterrence followed by diplomacy was needed by Singapore for its survival. This pattern is also followed by many smaller nations and non-nuclear countries. Singapore had always paid attention to the balance of power rather than seeking an international power to act as a protector for extended deterrence.

There is also another notable aspect of deterrence development in the smaller non-nuclear states. These nations were separated from a larger neighbouring country or usually recognised by their larger neighbours only to make their national security concerns directed towards the acts of their parent country or neighbouring ones. For example, one of Singapore's long-term concerns has always been securing its sea routes from its maritime neighbour and parent- Malaysia. The example of Singapore's deterrence is specifically unique in nature as it is the only country to do so. Singapore keeps on strengthening its inland defence capabilities making it more powerful although being smaller when compared to its neighbours. The nation also showed massive feats in economic accomplishments. Singapore became the hub for entrepot trade making its economy more self-reliant and stronger.

Singapore also implemented good aspects of psychological deterrence. The nation's enlistment acts state that all the male citizens and permanent residents (PRs) of Singapore is liable to national service obligations. This in turn increased the nation's pride and uniqueness among its larger neighbours. Thus, the nation constantly invests heavily in its defence, economic, and civil aspects making it a country not to mess with. Thus, Singapore's inland deterrence concept can be matched with deterrence by denial. Those nations who thinks to mess with Singapore backs off since they realise their plans do not turn fruitful if implemented.

Another example can be found in the case of China and Japan in their political use of the Taiwan card. As stated earlier although the Communist Party of China threatened to use nuclear bombs against Japan if it shows further interference in the Taiwan issue, but still the call for nuclear strikes was prevented. So, Japan is a non-nuclear state and with no offensive military capabilities relies heavily on the United States for its external (national) security. Thus, if all the scenario for nuclear strikes arises from China it will be a serious international issue along with the involvement of US armed forces in launching a full-scale attack against China with the use of nuclear bombs. Also, the Senkaku Islands/Diaoyutai Qundao dispute made Japan clear in its stance on using the deterrence by punishment strategy.

Both China and Japan will remain hostile constantly in the upcoming years regarding the island dispute, Japan's self-defence navy forces have taken serious moves to safeguard the maritime routes to the Senkaku Islands/Diaoyutai Qundao thus cutting off the Chinese navy from occupying further. This shows a clear-cut response to China, that if it proceeds further Japan could escalate the tensions much higher.

From a broader perspective, conventional deterrence strategies are proved on much weaker theoretical grounds in comparison to nuclear deterrence. The outcomes of deterrence strategies removing the nuclear component are less predictable and more subject-able to long-run strategic miscalculations. Thus, non-nuclear states will have no panacea when compared to nations driven by nuclear stuffing. On the other hand, the proclamation of Churchill's beliefs stated above indeed holds till today as no nation even went to the brink of a nuclear conflict or war. In the upcoming decades too, no nation could choose nuclear conflict to settle for peace. Thus, when looking on to overlay skins of deterrence strategies pursued by both nuclear states and as well as non-nuclear states, they land on a solution where everyone benefits.

When the entire world shook over the invention of nuclear weapons creating a domain of superior advantage over winning a war, there emerged a new domain of space which added another whole new dimension to the dynamics of warfare itself. The introduction of electronic communications and computers paved way for warfare techniques from the battlefield to the virtual battle-space. As crucial papers were made in electronic form and stored in data format there emerged a new concept of data protection. Thus, in border aspects, a nation's security agencies were pushed to develop a cyber deterrence strategy. The aspects of cyber deterrence exactly match with that of traditional deterrence- a credible defence, the ability to retaliate, and the will to retaliate. The concept of cyber deterrence builds upon this strategy to alter an adversary's actions for fear of an impossible counteraction. Many cyber experts and military engineers argue the viability of cyber deterrence. Some of the arguments which make cyber deterrence the least priority are as follows.

Building a cyber realm incurs a heavy cost to the governments. Cyber security is an expensive business and a difficult strategy to develop and master. Taking a closer look at the United States' defence budget in recent times, the nation has invested US$10 million for every 125 lines of offensive codes developed. Although this expensive investment was not put into use in any cyber conflicts for the US, it indeed proved US' massive cyber warfare capabilities. In the case of cyber war against the United States, the nation has more chances of bagging an easy victory. In addition to this, other reports claim that countries like Pakistan, India, China, and Iran are also developing massive cyber warfare capabilities.

Image Credit: Yahoo News

In a broader perspective, deterrence in the cyber realm may seem like a complete component but the pillars needed to support the strategy of cyber deterrence are yet to be identified, especially the pillars like the will to retaliate and the ability to retaliate. Unlike the traditional means of warfare where the attacker remains visible, in the cyber realm the attacker often called a 'hacker' remains buried in electronic shadows. In many cases, it becomes impossible for security agencies to crack the encryption layers of the hacker. For example, the Stuxnet computer worm which was targeted to compromise and expose Iran's nuclear weapons program exemplifies the difficulty for government agencies to trace down who the real attacker was. No concrete evidence was collected to prove that the worm originated either from the US or Israel.

So, for cyber deterrence to work, potential attackers must be sufficiently fed up with the fear of their identity being exposed and retaliation in form of punishment could be carried against them. If a nation fails to identify who the hacker was, then retaliation is not possible which is a vital component of deterrence doctrine. Thus, the deterrence in the cyber realm nullifies making the cyber domain a pure form of business. The cyber security firms provide security layers to their customers who pay them while the same line of codes used in security software is exploited by hackers later only to monetise those exploitations to cyber security organisations. Thus, it creates a chain of business rather than a domain of warfare.

The ability to retaliate in case of a cyber-attack is minimal. So, those who want to retaliate must repeatedly do so to create cyber deterrence. The constant security patches and updates make it even more difficult to trace the origin of the attack. The current set of international laws applies to cyber warfare off the records thus, lacking a legal framework. The unclear legal status of cyber laws makes it a challenge for countries to enforce the will to retaliate. It drives a nation to develop its priorities toward conventional deterrence strategies. With the advent of free educational resources, even an individual can equip himself/herself with enough technical knowledge to handle computers and perform network penetration tests. In other words, even a small group of people (non-state actors) can also launch a cyber-attack against any nation. Black hat groups such as LulzSec and Anonymous are notable examples of non-state actors who carried out some of the most damaging cyber-attacks.

The involvement of non-state actors further complicates the development of cyber deterrence. Their involvement creates the notion for governments to retaliate against them are worth the shot. In the worst case, non-state actors sometimes are hired by government agencies to launch an attack against their neighbouring states or an enemy state. In such cases, strong immunity is provided to those non-state actor groups making the will to retaliate result in failure.

All these criteria make the cyber realm as a form of viable deterrence package, a difficult one to achieve. In the current scenario, cyber deterrence is non-viable to practice due to the involvement of many obstacles like diminishing capability to retaliate, non-state actors, existing legal issues, ability and will to retaliate etc. The incurring costs to develop a huge cyber realm to form cyber deterrence later only to keep it in a virtual notion makes several countries dissuade from adopting this strategy. As cyber deterrence predominantly focuses on the ability to retaliate and the will to retaliate which are important skills that nations must be able to master if they go for developing virtual warfare capabilities. So, developing a cyber deterrence strategy is both risky and problematic. Unless the nation is willing to spend billions of dollars for technology providing speed speed attribution or until international norms of cyber warfare are established, this form as a means of deterrence will remain just penned as academic papers/journals.

Given today's technology having a credible and robust super-computer is the only viable approach toward building cyber deterrence.

There is another dynamic of warfare which is emerging with the advent of COVID-19. The so-called deadly pandemic made certain nations' economies boom while others fall behind a few decades. Nations have learned to leverage COVID-19 to establish economic deterrence. This type of deterrence can be defined as 'efforts utilising economic threats to discourage the deterred state's military aggression. Stronger economies achieve this by manipulating cost-benefit expectations of military aggression.

During this pandemic, Europe's economy received a more lethal blow when compared to other regions of the world. Even beyond the military domain, Europe's weakness was easily exploited by Russia and China. These two communist nations proved to be immune to the virus themselves and exploited the European markets at their best. China positioned itself as the alternative provider of soft power, while the United States was barely able to handle the crisis.

Using economic deterrence via imposing economic sanctions has become one of the favourite tools for the governments to respond to foreign economic policy challenges. The sanctions can be in form of impositions such as travel bans, assets freeze, arms embargoes, and trade locks (restrictions). All these tools have been implemented by many countries during the ongoing pandemic. For example, Singapore imposed a travel ban to and from not only India but also its neighbouring countries. In 2019, the United States imposed comprehensive sanctions on Cuba, North Korea, Iran, Sudan, and Syria to cripple some suspected activities of crimes and trafficking. The assets were also blocked to cut off cargo movement into these countries.

The world bank has long time blacklisted Pakistan from securing funds through its members. This sanction enabled to curb the crime rates in Pakistan Occupied Kashmir (POK) as the world bank found that funds were directly channelised towards terrorist organisations operating from that region. Recently economically stronger nations like the UK and the US cut off trade relations with the Islamic Emirate of Afghanistan where the country is under Taliban rule. With all these under usage do the nations get credible results by deploying strategies of economic deterrence?

Image Credit: Global Times

Many desk experts and real-time economists suggest that economic sanctions, especially targeted and well-planned sanctions will be successful but only in long term. It should remain in the government's toolbox for a very long period. Impositions which are generally well planned with a specific objective end up being successful. Furthermore, these sanctions may achieve desired results but not change the behaviour all the time. Sanctions often evolve to be successful over time. For example, as stated above sanctions on the Islamic Emirate of Afghanistan would create solid results only after a certain amount of time has passed out. It takes Afghanistan under the Taliban's rule to run out of all the essential resources only to later surrender to major powers like the US.

However, the scope of these measures can change even in the opposite direction over time. The comparative utility of sanctions is what matters, not simply whether they have achieved their objective. The main advantage of economic sanctions is their credibility and flexibility. The target usually is weaker in terms of economy and self-reliance fears that sanctions may be imposed more severe. For example, the Obama administration responded to major political reforms that occurred in Myanmar back in 2012. Once again when the country started abusing Rohingya minority people, the US once again put strict impositions against Myanmar.

The policymakers of a country must keep in mind to use economic sanctions very carefully as it's a double-edged sword. If used without proper planning, it can lead to backfire for the nation in the long run. In the Post-COVID era, the world will have a permanent dependence on more of a kind of economic warfare. In the 21st century, the world has not witnessed any full-scale war yet. So, in the upcoming decades, the same is applicable. Nations would prefer to use more economic deterrence to achieve their goals and objectives. Thus, economic sanctions as a form of deterrence strategy are more viable as it yields successful result to achieve diplomatic goals.

The definition of state proposed by William Olson is;

".... a legal and territorial expression, involving a population politically organised under one government in one place with sovereign rights, even though it may have possessions elsewhere."

Upon closer analysis, one can understand that the fundamental driving force of states is to protect their sovereignty at any cost. Those costs range from the very basic struggle for survival of the nation (both material and ideological). Thus, these forces drive a nation to give utmost priority to peace, and security, preserve sovereignty and attain its goals. Thus, each nation being unique (in terms of geography, ethnicity, language, politics, ideology etc) is bound to have its own goals and objectives. To achieve their desired goals nations sometimes need to bump into each other in terms of war. Thus, the most rational way to ensure national security is by deploying deterrence strategies- whether by accumulating power internally or aligning with external forces. Because of the constant security dilemma like hunger for a world superpower label, nations constantly go for developing the most advanced weapon systems to increase their deterrence capabilities. Thus, **nuclear deterrence remains an all-weather ally** in case of maximum military capabilities in the current scenario. As nations race towards protecting themselves by any means puts the notion of power as a multi-dimensional complex structure.

Some analysts argue that economic power has replaced military power as a central means of international relations while other experts still rely upon the traditional means of deterrence- military capabilities. By the end of the day, military power speaks huge than economic sanctions. For example, during the Gulf war strictest economic sanctions were imposed on Iraq but still, the nation did not move an inch out of Kuwait until America took multi-nation military action. It was the use of force here to resolve the conflict. The governments should learn when to use economic deterrence. For example, Singapore or ASEAN cannot stop Indonesia from burning its forests while Finland cannot stop Russia from emitting huge amounts of sulphur dioxides. Thus, nations can collaborate to impose strong economic sanctions against countries involved in environmental issues.

Diplomacy is itself as old as deterrence. One should not confuse that both relate the same. Diplomacy is the starting point of showing deterrence by any nation. Nations surviving in the 21st century have themselves subscribed not only to deterrence but also to its child instruments such as diplomacy, collective security and Cooperation. In conclusion, deterrence strategies are still viable in the 21st century. Running into the 3rd decade of this century world has not seen any major conflicts like full-scale wars. This is due to only implementing deterrence strategies by major powers of the world. **Thus, it can be concluded that deterrence strategies are viable in the 21st century.**

References & Endnotes

1. "Bernard Brodie (Military Strategist)." Wikipedia, 18 Sept. 2022, en.wikipedia.org/wiki?curid=2136884.
2. Martens, Simba. "Book Review: Deterrence in the 21st Century – Insights from Theory and Practice." HCSS, 3 May 2021, hcss.nl/news/book-review-deterrence-in-the-21st-century-insights-from-theory-and-practice/.
3. "Deterrence | Definition of Deterrence by Oxford Dictionary on Lexico.com Also Meaning of Deterrence." Lexico Dictionaries | English, www.lexico.com/definition/deterrence.

4. "Read 'Post-Cold War Conflict Deterrence' at NAP.edu." Www.nap.edu, www.nap.edu/read/5464/chapter/5.

5. Weitz, Richard. "Why to Give North Korea Food Aid." Thediplomat.com, thediplomat.com/2011/09/why-to-give-north-korea-food-aid/.

6. readJuly 19, Jonathan TalbotDeputy Editor3 min, and 2021 - 12:42PM. "CCP Sanctioned Video Threatens China Will Nuke Japan." Skynews, 19 July 2021, www.skynews.com.au/world-news/china/ccp-sanctioned-video-threatens-china-will-nuke-japan-in-a-fullscale-war/news-story/dd3ce2fdab6e83fa77025eb5c3d23803.

7. Zhao, Toby Dalton, Tong, and Toby Dalton Zhao Tong. "At a Crossroads? China-India Nuclear Relations after the Border Clash." Carnegie Endowment for International Peace, carnegieendowment.org/2020/08/19/at-crossroads-china-india-nuclear-relations-after-border-clash-pub-82489.

8. "Cuba." The Nuclear Threat Initiative, www.nti.org/learn/countries/cuba/#:~:text=Cuba%20is%20not%20known%20to. Accessed 17 Oct. 2022.

9. "Quoteland.com :: Tell a Friend." Www.quoteland.com, www.quoteland.com/share/Sir-Winston-Churchill-Quotes/9271/. Accessed 17 Oct. 2022.

10. http://bitly.ws/vvns

11. "Introduction." SCDF, www.scdf.gov.sg/home/ns-matters/cd-nsf/introduction. Accessed 17 Oct. 2022.

12. Wu, Shang-Su. "A Comparative Study of the National Defence Policies of Singapore and Taiwan between 1965 and 2008." Unsworks.unsw.edu.au, 2012, unsworks.unsw.edu.au/fapi/datastream/unsworks:10775/SOURCE01?view=true.

13. "Situation of the Senkaku Islands." Ministry of Foreign Affairs of Japan, www.mofa.go.jp/a_o/c_m1/senkaku/page1we_000010.html.

14. "The Challenges of Cyber Deterrence - PDF Free Download." Docplayer.net, docplayer.net/10626697-The-challenges-of-cyber-deterrence.html. Accessed 17 Oct. 2022.

15. http://bitly.ws/vvnM

16. Oup.com, 2022, academic.oup.com/fpa/article-abstract/15/2/176/4939180?redirectedFrom=fulltext.

17. "Deterrence and Defense in Times of COVID-19 | DGAP." Dgap.org, dgap.org/en/research/publications/deterrence-and-defense-times-covid-19. Accessed 17 Oct. 2022.

18. Masters, Jonathan. "What Are Economic Sanctions?" Council on Foreign Relations, 12 Aug. 2019, www.cfr.org/backgrounder/what-are-economic-sanctions.

19. ANI. "Firms Blacklisted by World Bank Got CPEC Contracts: Alice Wells." Business Standard India, 22 Jan. 2020, www.business-standard.com/article/news-ani/firms-blacklisted-by-world-bank-got-cpec-contracts-alice-wells-120012200406_1.html.

CHAPTER III

Indian Ocean Security

The Indian Ocean occupies a position of unique geo-strategic importance amid the maritime arenas of the world. The earliest networks of inter-regional, cross-border interaction between East and West were made directly possible by the compact, closed character of the Indian Ocean geography. But evolving dynamics of governance, commerce, demography, knowledge and religion in what has always been a cosmopolitan arena, together with shifting patterns of collaboration and conflict in an interestingly interconnected world, are today compounded by energy security and in environmental concerns that dominate any meaningful contemporary analyses of region. The Indo-Pacific maritime space has acquired fresh strategic significance in the post-Cold war era and the present epoch of globalisation and nuclearisation, especially with the economic renaissance of East Asia and the concurrent rise of India & China.

Post 9/11, maritime security issues in the Indian Ocean region have also been amplified by the expanding context of a transnational war against terrorism. The dawn of the 21st century has ushered in a vital phase of globalised maritime trade via dense sea-lanes of communication; a spectrum of as asymmetric conflicts across maritime and littoral domains; and a host of other challenges in traditional and non-traditional areas of maritime security. The essays under this chapter analyse exposition and issues of maritime order, littoral security; great power strategic competition in the Indian Ocean Region; issues of nuclear weapons; maritime access and basing; energy security; sea-based asymmetric threats; and arms trafficking (including of mass destruction). The subject matter reviews issues of maritime security cooperation and the role of navies in addressing transnational and asymmetric threats as well as performing humanitarian and constabulary functions.

The essays were written carefully after reviewing and studying the following stated below. Also the essays aim to provide a structured overview and systematic analysis of the crucial issues of Indian Ocean Security;

- The geo-strategic significance of the Indian Ocean and its wider relationship to Southeast Asia and East Asia.

- The scope of maritime security issues in the Indian Ocean Region, whether competitive, co-operative, or convergent in character.
- The interplay between forces of globalisation and maritime power in the Indian Ocean region.
- The sources of asymmetric conflict in the maritime domain- piracy, terrorism, and other challenges to good order at sea.
- Importance of coastal security as a factor of maritime security in the Indian Ocean region.
- Significance of nuclear weapons as well as the maritime transit of weapons of mass destruction and fissile nuclear materials across the region.
- Spectrum of issues arising from multinational maritime engagements in the Indian Ocean region, with implications for maritime security cooperation.

• • •

Colombo Security Conclave: Is it a new Minilateral hostile to China in the Indian Ocean?

(A version of this following article was published in Khabarhub- a digital media owned by PAVILION MEDIA PVT LTD located at Kathmandu, Nepal)

The Colombo Security Conclave (CSC) was hosted virtually by Sri Lanka from its headquarters in Colombo in early August. A meeting of top-ranking officials such as deputy national security advisors (DNSAs) from Sri Lanka, India, and the Maldives along with high-ranking government officials from observer nations of the CSC. This unique conclave deliberated security cooperation across "four pillars" namely maritime security, human trafficking, counterterrorism, and disaster management. The observer nations, namely Bangladesh, Maturities, and Seychelles are set to become permanent members of the Colombo Security Conclave at the next national security level meeting scheduled to take place in the Maldives later this year.

The CSC's ambition is very clear. The emergence of the Indian Ocean Region as the new strategic battle arena comes along with its demerits too. Widening security concerns of sea piracy, goods (including drugs and arms) smuggling, controlling illegal entry into strategic sea lanes, combating maritime pollution and cyber security are some of the intersecting worries for the CSC nations.

Image Credit: The Hindu

Another outstanding cause for reviving this security conclave back to life was the aggressive maritime policy implemented by China in the Indian Ocean. Maritime policy behaviour of China towards the Indian Ocean is seen as a constant emerging threat by both permanent as well as current observer CSC nations. In late October 2020, Beijing held its fifth plenary session which deliberated upon the 11th five-year plan and the 2035 grand vision of the Chinese Communist Party.

The plenary session emphasised expanding the domestic market based on consumption & innovation. China's ambition as stated in the grand vision makes it strengthen its foothold in the Indian Ocean Region stretching from Djibouti in Africa to far East Asia beyond the South China Sea. Since 2020, the dragon's aggressive advancements in the sea, especially in the Indian Ocean resulted in an eye-opener for India, Sri Lanka, and Bangladesh. Thus, the trilateral level National Security Advisors (NSAs) came back into action as Colombo Security Conclave which, was held in November 2020, the latter being in limbo since 2014.

In the aftermath of the meeting, there was an uproar among South Asian scholars that CSC must stay clear of the current QUAD-China face-offs. Although the revival of the trilateral meeting was an Indian effort, Scholars say that India should not bring long-rooted rivalry with China into the platform. Though Scholars debate the CSC should transcend beyond QUAD-China clashes and must serve as a personal subregional forum for combating non-traditional security concerns among its members. Upon deeper probing into the latter statement, the following facts would put why the Colombo Security Conclave must give equal priority to considering the China debate.

China's ambitious One Belt One Road (OBOR) project created a fulcrum to leverage trillions of dollars of government loans and state-owned industries' investments across Italy till the South China Sea and resulted in returns falling back into China. The OBOR is regarded as a serious threat by India as it breaks land sovereignty (of India) across the Indo-China Himalayan border, which in turn, has resulted in numerous border incursions, standoffs, and clashes since 2000. A part of OBOR project execution in peninsular India, which gave rise to the infamous maritime strategy (of China) known as the String of Pearls resulted in serious damages in the past to the current CSC member nations.

The string of pearls strategy paved a clear route for China to encircle India in its peninsular region. Today the communist giant has or is building deep-water ports in Sri Lanka, Pakistan, an oil-gas pipeline in Myanmar and in Aksai Chin (China Occupied Kashmir), and a military logistic base in Djibouti. Unable to pay Chinese loans, these nations later fall into the debt trap. The classic example of the latter case is when Sri Lanka was forced to China's 99-year lease of its Hambantota Port region. It shows, China was using OBOR imitative to implement debt-trap diplomacy. After loading struggling economies with debt, they cannot repay, China leverages its role as a creditor to coerce them into ceding control over strategically important ports, resources, and commercial routes. Apart from Gwadar port (Baluchistan, Pakistan) and the Hambantota port which already fell victim to the dragon's realpolitik, littoral islands like Maldives and nations in the IOR region are most exposed to the Chinese debt trap with an exception being India. Thus, looking at past India failed in the race in winning the hands of Sri Lanka and the Maldives against China due to its poor strategic forecast.

Sri Lanka, Bangladesh, Maldives, and other nations don't want to join an organisation that may be perceived as overtly Anti-China. This is the fact that the CSC formerly NSAs remained in limbo right after its establishment in early 2011.

Bangladesh and Sri Lanka in recent times have shown clear advancements in isolating themselves from the wicked encirclement strategies of China. The dragon's potential port and oil pipeline project in Bangladesh has shown no progress to date and is thus considered a failed one, but still China under Xi-Jinping's administration has not given up the venture. As noticeable in the case of Djibouti where China established its only overseas military base, Bangladesh has not allowed Chinese investments in their deep port projects as it will lead to a suitable naval base for China to gain an immediate gateway into the Bay of Bengal. Unlike Sri Lanka and Pakistan, Bangladesh executed prudent macro-economic management to not fall into the Chinese debt trap. However, Paulo Casaca founder of the South Asia Democratic Forum stated in his writings that the Bangladesh government has been relatively careless of their participation in BRI which brought potential geopolitical dependency on the communist giant.

The volume of investments made by China in Bangladesh makes it the second most valuable component of OBOR after Gwadar in Pakistan. China tried to interfere in the internal matters of Bangladesh influenced them not to engage with India and western powers such as the United States.

From an Indian perspective, the elephant sees sub-regional engagement like the CSC as critical for securing its strategic interests. The expansion of CSC's membership indicates widening areas of cooperation and the growing convergence among Indian Ocean Region nations to work together on a common platform thus deepening their engagement under a regional framework. Moreover, The South Asian Association for Regional Cooperation (SAARC) has not made an exemplary feat in recent times. All other major sub-regional alliances are being a stalemate. Thus, the revival of CSC proved to reflect the new Minilateral heading towards enhancing sub-regional diplomacy, which India has attempted to foster in the neighbourhood to keep Chinese advancements at bay.

Soon, India through the CSC might look forward to sharing defence technologies, increasing its naval presence in the Indian Ocean (in its backyard), and strengthening overseas investments in the CSC member nations especially littoral states like Maldives, Mauritius, and Seychelles. Through the CSC, the littoral member nations not only might transform into a navy anchor hub for India but also strengthen their domestic maritime security as these littoral nations possess a tiny navy unit. This will open fast travel portals for the navy units in the Indian Ocean, thus keeping a due check on Chinese patrol units. The Colombo Security Conclave is a way forward in establishing an unbreakable security bond in the Indian Ocean.

References & Endnotes

1. "Colombo Security Conclave: A New Minilateral for the Indian Ocean?" Thedilomat.com, thediplomat.com/2021/08/colombo-security-conclave-a-new-minilateral-for-the-indian-ocean/. Accessed 17 Oct. 2022.

2. "Welcome to High Commission of India, Colombo, Sri Lanka." http://bitly.ws/vvJH. Accessed 17 Oct. 2022.

3. "Bangladesh, Mauritius and Seychelles to Join Regional Maritime Security Grouping." Hindustan Times, 9 Aug. 2021, www.hindustantimes.com/india-news/bangladesh-mauritius-and-seychelles-to-join-regional-maritime-security-grouping-101628503515228.html. Accessed 17 Oct. 2022.

4. Briefing, China. "Reading China's Vision 2035 Plan: Megacities, Trade, Market Consumption." China Briefing News, 24 Mar. 2021, www.china-briefing.com/news/chinas-vision-2035-from-beijings-forbidden-city-to-interconnected-eurasian-megacity/.

5. "4th NSA Level Meeting on Trilateral Maritime Security Cooperation." Mea.gov.in, mea.gov.in/press-releases.htm?dtl/33238/4th_NSA_Level_Meeting_on_Trilateral_Maritime_Security_Cooperation. Accessed 17 Oct. 2022.

6. Rashid, Mufassir. "Colombo Security Conclave: Bangladesh's Perspective – OpEd." Eurasia Review, 17 Aug. 2021, www.eurasiareview.com/17082021-colombo-security-conclave-bangladeshs-perspective-oped/.

7. "The String of Pearls vs the Iron Curtain; by Anirudh Ramakrishna Phadke." The Viyug, 24 Mar. 2019, viyug.com/2019/03/24/the-string-of-pearls-vs-the-iron-curtain-by-anirudh-ramakrishna-phadke/. Accessed 17 Oct. 2022.

8. "China's Security Gambit in the Indian Ocean | EastWest Institute." Eastwest.ngo, 2020, www.eastwest.ngo/idea/china%E2%80%99s-security-gambit-indian-ocean. Accessed 17 Oct. 2022.

9. Stashwick, Steven. "China's Security Gambit in the Indian Ocean." Thediplomat.com, thediplomat.com/2018/05/chinas-security-gambit-in-the-indian-ocean/. Accessed 17 Oct. 2022.

10. "China, Bangladesh Sign Framework Agreement on Oil Pipeline Project - Xinhua | English.news.cn." Www.xinhuanet.com, www.xinhuanet.com/english/2017-10/30/c_136713614.htm. Accessed 17 Oct. 2022.

11. "Bangladesh Resists 'Debt-Trap' of China, Avoids BRI Heavy-Handedness." Mint, 11 July 2021, www.livemint.com/news/world/bangladesh-resists-debt-trap-of-china-avoids-belt-and-road-initiative-heavyhandedness-11625962332098.html.

12. "India Revives Maritime Security Bloc with an Eye on China's Growing Influence." South China Morning Post, 17 Aug. 2021, www.scmp.com/week-asia/politics/article/3145256/india-revives-indian-ocean-security-bloc-eye-chinas-growing.

• • •

Finding Deterrence Strategies Deployed in the Indian Ocean Region

Introduction

The Indian Ocean is the third largest water body and covers 20% of the earth's surface after the Pacific and the Atlantic Oceans. In the current century it has become the most viable sea route for trade and commerce connecting the US from the West to Australia in the East. This vast theatre of water stretches from the Strait of Malacca and Australia's western coast in the East to the Mozambique Channel in the West. This region serves as a home to key locations such as the Arabian Sea, Bay of Bengal, Straits, Islands of Africa, and Islands of India, and is surrounded by power players of current global order such as China and India.

Serving livelihoods to around 2.5 billion people, the region's vastness and diversity speak of its geostrategic importance. The vital trading and business potential of this region paved way for wars between colonial powers such as the British, French, and Portuguese to establish a monopoly over this region to reap its luxurious benefits. Furthermore, the end of the Cold War era created a new geopolitical framework for the 'Indian Ocean Region.' Thus, at the heart of the geopolitical struggle, different major powers from the colonial era till today have constant military presence along with various means of deterrence strategies deployed in the Indian Ocean to maintain a sense of geopolitical stability.

For example, Kanhoji Angria a Maratha Navy Admiral was famous for his marvellous naval warfare capabilities who deployed excellent sea deterrence strategies and injected the fear of serious punishments in the hearts of the British and Portuguese for exploiting India during the British era. He was dubbed as the 'master of the Arabian Sea.' In Today's scenario global powers such as India, China, and the US are engaged in the race for dominance in the Indian Ocean Region. Thus, this paper attempts to find the various means of deterrence strategies used and can be used in the Indian Ocean with a special focus on India and China.

Under-Sea Nuclear Deterrence

Image Credit: Business Insider

The acronym SSBN representing nuclear-powered ballistic missile submarine is considered one of the most destructive weapons currently roaming in the waters of the Indian Ocean. These submarines are gone undetected thus being dubbed invulnerable to attacks. The introduction of these weapons has changed the dynamics of undersea warfare by adding the nuclear (total annihilation) component. Currently, the United States have 14 SSBNs, China runs with 6 SSBNs and finally India with one and only SSBN called INS Arihant (S3) which was commissioned in 2016. Although the US have a higher number of SSBNs serious competition arises since China has a much stronger foothold in the Indian Ocean region than the latter democratic giant.

China's wider strategic activity and 2030 vision of controlling East Asia have deepened the concerns of many countries, especially those engulfed around the Indian Ocean Region. Despite several warnings from US Pentagon, India's Ministry of External Affairs (MEA) and other nations' concerned authorities, China has been increasing its aggressive advancements which have resulted in several obvious flashcards such as territorial disputes in the South & East China Sea with Japan and Taiwan and unhealthy competition with India in the Indian Ocean.

Many of these flashcards are accompanied by calls for nuclear threats from China itself to keep its enemies at bay. One credible explanation that the Chinese administration gives us is that they have concerns regarding threats from US' permanent military presence in the Indian Ocean and the South China Sea which create hurdles for China to freely practice trade and sea exploration. Thus, as a means of deterrence China aims to make that region an SSBNs populated area. Another credible reason China gives is that the nation can possess diplomatic turbulences with India over Maldives' treatment, as both the nation's outlook towards the tiny Island differs.

Another credible reason for China establishing undersea deterrence by being willing to increase the population of its SSBNs is due to the recent AUKUS (Australia United Kingdom US) pact. Under this new security pact, the US and Britain will provide full assistance to Australia including the technology to build nuclear-powered submarines. Although Australian Prime Minister Morrison said the nation is seeking to establish civil nuclear capability, China has delivered its sharp dislike to this pact. China's foreign ministry spokesperson Zhao Lijian said that the treaty will affect regional stability, intensifies the arms race, and downplays international non-proliferation efforts.

Commodore Venugopal Menon (retd) says that AUKUS will keep China busy with Pacific theatre which will result in the reduction of the threat level posed by China in the Indian Ocean. This creates ample time for India to revive its Under-Sea warfare capabilities and rise stronger in the coming years.

Given this potential threat of China deploying more SSBNs intersecting with Indian interests, India will be more likely to strengthen its naval nuclear capabilities. Apart from INS Arihant, India will commission another SSBN named 'INS Arighat' in near future, having sea trials in a completed stage. Although India sees Pakistan as a mere proxy in the maritime realm, still the nation does not downplay its (Pakistan) nuclear naval implementation. Pakistan established a Naval Strategic Command Force to implement nuclear-powered submarines to develop its sea deterrence doctrine, which is once again fully backed up by China.

Thus, Pakistan's 'First Use' nuclear doctrine and willingness to develop a sea deterrence made growing concerns for India to speed up the process of deploying a second SSBN in the Indian Ocean. This will further enable India to strengthen its nuclear doctrine- second strike capabilities. Currently, India does not possess good land-based nuclear deterrence capabilities. In the case of China, the communist giant can deploy missiles easily into populated territory close to India's border across the Himalayas whereas in the case of India it can barely reach the populated territory of the eastern part of China with its nuclear technologies.

Given these constraints, India develops a powerful undersea deterrence and with the given technology it can deploy its SSBN either in the Bay of Bengal or deep into the southern parts of the Indian Ocean. The US also has a significant role in facilitating nuclear stability in this region. In recent times the US has shown good signs by supporting India's maritime nuclear doctrine as well as showing interest in Pakistan's attempt to establish nuclear submarines. This sign would be critical in stabilising the India-Pakistan nuclear dynamic. Nevertheless, a potentially more dangerous risk of tensions and escalations awaits in the Indian Ocean in the coming days.

Security Dialogues as a form of Sea-going Deterrent

Many international forums and security dialogues were established to promote stability and free & open trade in the Indian Ocean. One such famous security dialogue named QUAD (Quadrilateral Security Dialogue) always fall into the hands of critics and commentators calling it an **'Asian NATO'** and stalemate despite its members having several meetings. The QUAD has been criticised for having its sole purpose to deter China in the

Indian & Pacific Oceans, **which is indeed true**. China's rapid modernisation has made huge concerns for India as the nation feels many parts of its sea routes especially in the Indian Ocean have been breached.

Originally this security dialogue was born instantly out of the 2004 Indian tsunami disaster that occurred in Tamil Nadu in a notion of countering natural calamities, today QUAD's goal has changed due to changes in the dynamics of the geopolitical framework in the Indian Ocean Region. Thus, returning from QUAD 2.0 in 2017, the members re-framed their goals and objectives given the military modernisation challenges posed by China. Today QUAD's objectives include regular military exercises with the recent example, of being Malabar military exercise and the long-term goal- to upgrade this security dialogue as a fully functional alternative to China's Belt Road Initiative.

The QUAD grouping has met bi-annually since their realignment of goals to discuss connectivity, sustainable development, counterterrorism, non-proliferation, and maritime and cyber security to promote peace and stability in the Indian Ocean Region. Thus, QUAD members set out to challenge China in its own game, creating a self-reliant atmosphere to cut off heavy Chinese exports to other countries. US has shown an improved sign-in setting up its market in India thereby making China cut off its debt trap diplomacy to BRI (Belt and Road Initiative) and its child initiatives.

This counterstrategy has not yet fully evolved, but each of the QUAD member countries has shown good cooperation and coordination in their responses to execute the proposed plans, for example, US coordination in South Asia and the Indian Ocean Region with India. The QUAD never downplays the notion of military dimension. India has further strengthened its naval ties with other QUAD members and there have been more interactions on political and military levels including both formal and informal dialogues.

Another kind of security dialogue, more of a regional perspective meant only for the Indian Ocean named 'The Colombo Security Conclave' (CSC) has been once again pumped back into life by New Delhi in early August this year. Analysts see this as a crucial move for India to secure its strategic interests in the Indian Ocean. As of the present date, the CSC is the only active subregional forum in the Indian Ocean Region. The Deputy National Security Advisors (DNSAs) from India, Sri Lanka, and the tiny island nation- Maldives met virtually at a conference hosted by Sri Lanka along with Bangladesh, Mauritius, and Seychelles in an observer status. The

DNSAs discussed the four pillars namely cyber security, maritime security, counterterrorism, and human trafficking in the Indian Ocean. Desk experts see China as a significant driver for India's motive to revitalise the Colombo Security Conclave back into form.

Image Credit: The Quint

One of the outcomes of the conclave was to upgrade observer nations' status into permanent members. The logic in this move is that by joining more members India can have support to balance its stiff competition with China in the Indian Ocean. The Indian government has constant worries due to a report stating that China's navy (PLAN) is in the process to establish a '**special naval fleet for the Indian Ocean**'. On the other hand, China through its BRI project has constantly attempted to gain the hands of every other country in the Indian Ocean except India.

China's only operational (foreign) military base in Djibouti has given such a strategic advantage. The communist nation gets full access into the backyard of the Arabian Sea and its functional port in Gwadar, Pakistan makes it a complete civil-military balance (presence) for China in the Indian Ocean. Also, China has been sending its warships inside the Indian waters of the Exclusive Economic Zone (EEZ) which is located near the Andaman and Nicobar Islands. This reminds India to further heighten its military in its backyard- the Indian Ocean.

Thus, the China debate is an important agenda for India, the democratic Asian power under Prime Minister Modi's administration showed full resistance to China by growing the framework of the CSC. India also has been constantly improving its diplomatic relationship with each of the CSC members individually to further strengthen its success parameters. In the race to gain the hands of the tiny island nations such as Mauritius and Seychelles, India once again overtakes China by providing them aid, and human and material capacities.

Thus, upon close probing into the international & regional security dialogues, India and its allies have been trying to create a convenient form of sea deterrence. This would result in the outcome being more reliable than nuclear deterrence. The latter is considered a lender of last resort and most of the nations having interests in the Indian Ocean Region such as the US, India, China, and Pakistan are all nuclear capable countries with developed nuclear doctrines. Moreover, these countries have realised going for nuclear attacks would disable them since nuclear is a weapon of total annihilation. So, countries have adopted the method of mounting nuclear weapons in the navy and prefer security dialogues for a more reliable source of Seagoing deterrence.

China's Economic & Military Deterrence in the Indian Ocean

Scholars trace the roots of Chinese non-combat operations in the Indian Ocean starting long back into 1991 when the concerned authorities sent state-owned rescue vessels to bring back stranded Chinese citizens in Somalia. That is where when the world saw the capabilities of China conducting non-combat operations on deep seas. The 2006 Chinese white papers show that the nation has rising concerns over security-related issues about trade & commerce routes it had in the Indian Ocean. The 2008 defence white paper of China showed the world that given the rising competition in the Indian Ocean, the need raised for China to establish PLAN's capabilities to establish a permanent military presence in the waters of the Indian Ocean.

During that time, China possessed 13.71 per cent of global market shares for commercial purposes. Thus, through five meta missions China developed an economic deterrence strategy that was executed which is having long-term impacts now in the Indian Ocean Region. Those are;

- Conduct non-combat activities focused on securing Chinese interests elsewhere other than Mainland China which included investments and bolstering of the nation's soft power.
- Undertake counterterrorism activities, unilaterally and bilaterally against an organisation that is deemed as a threat to China.
- Collect intelligence against its key adversaries.
- Give economic aid to small island countries in the Indian Ocean Region.
- Enable functional operational bodies having the ability to deter, mitigate, or terminate state-sponsored interdiction trade bound towards China. For example, to hold crucial assets of the US and India in an event of a massive conflict.

To justify its blue water logistic capabilities and far shores military presence, China began its ambitious plan back in 2008 by implementing a series of counterpiracy operations in the Gulf of Aden which to date has been running successfully without any interruptions. The deployments were some of the surface vessels of PLAN including nuclear-powered submarines. China used more than a decade of such deployments to prove its development in blue water logistical capabilities. Further in the year 2017, China established a fully functional blue water logistical base in Djibouti, Africa which enabled it to project immense power in the IOR along with a permanent military presence. **Recent Chinese white papers have declared that the establishment of a base in China's move for seagoing deterrence against the US and India.** The base will additionally support peacekeeping missions, deep sea explorations, protection of its overseas citizens, and security for its BRI investments.

The PLAN has developed its economic fleet consisting of guided cruise missiles (Type 055), destroyers (Type 052C/D), Frigates (Type 054A) and six large amphibious transport docks (Type 071) which can house four helicopters and four air-cushioned landing crafts. It has also built its auxiliary vessels including oilers, salvage & rescue ships, onboard hospital vessels, and large transport vessels which are already roaming the waters of the Indian Ocean. Thus, Chinese imports and exports are heavily guarded by its fleet anchored at various short strategic locations in the IOR.

China is also investing in other opportunities via its state-owned corporations to support is special type overseas missions in the IOR. China has been doing this since the emergence of QUAD back in 2007. To deter the impact of QUAD, China has been working constantly to gain hold of strategic points to escape the impact of international security dialogues. The cleverest investment by China ever in the IOR is the China Pakistan Occupied Kashmir Economic Corridor (CPOKEC) which is in Gwadar, Pakistan. It has been such a strategic advantage to China that it has reduced vast costs in imports and exports for its nation. It has made Pakistan an all-weather ally by supplying them with defence and commercial supplies for two decades in a row.

Through the Gwadar port it has connected the nation to Djibouti port and other BRI establishments in Africa and beyond the South China Sea in the east. It has been considered one of the strongest strategic investments made by China, which India to this day has difficulty deter with. China conducts defence engagement in South Asia only with Pakistan and Bangladesh has been reduced now to the latter nation. China's security relationship has been robust with Sri Lanka since the nation gained immense support from Beijing during the mid-stages of the Cold War. Although India revitalised its diplomatic relationship with Sri Lanka through the Colombo Security Conclave, India failed to deter Chinese movements in gaining Hambantota port. Future political level talks between China and Sri Lanka will most likely occur.

China successfully deterred India's heavy defence (military) influence in Mauritius and Seychelles by financing major bridge and other infrastructure developments. China-focused more on developing the economy of all the tiny island nations in the IOR, thereby making them fall prone to its debt-trap diplomacy. The PLAN's capabilities and tempo of operating in the The IOR region is huger than that India's current capabilities. All these overseas ports and establishments will prove a benefit for China in long run. The PLAN has trained in Non-combatant Evacuation Operations (NEO) and these overseas establishments come into play here. During any emergency for China, its government will use the disposable humanitarian aid located at its commercial port holdings. Through this China also ultimately aims in increasing its goodwill in the IOR.

Secondly, China has been engaging in conducting military exercises with its all-weather ally most preferably Pakistan under its aegis of the Shanghai Cooperation Organisation (SCO). Much of its counterterrorism operations remain opaque to date but reports suggest that China does bilateral military exercises to process intelligence exchange. China has also reportedly formed a special task force for its counterterrorism missions abroad. China seeks to protect its foreign investments such as BRI which is prone to terrorist attacks.

China has engaged in the active deployment of military vessels disguised as civilian research vessels which collect information and process the data in form of oceanographic maps useful for civil defence sectors and as well as military planners. It has collected all tactical advantage information regarding the routes taken by US and Indian navy warships in the Indian Ocean. Also report suggests that Huawei, a proxy of China's PLA (PEOPLE S LIBERATION ARMY) has given access to huge chunks of information that pass through 5G network cables that were installed in the Indian Ocean Region.

China has created an unbreakable infrastructure in the IOR which creates huge hurdles for India and US in securing their strategic interests. Taking the context of traditional strategies of deterrence, that is;

- **Deterrence by Denial**: by infeasibility or doubt, deterrence by denial attempts to deter action by making it infeasible or unlikely to succeed, thereby denying the aggressor confidence in its accomplishment. and
- **Deterrence by Punishment**: Alternatively, deterrence through punishment threatens severe penalties in the event of an attack, such as nuclear escalation or severe economic sanctions.

Now the question arises- which deterrence suit for pursual by India in the Indian Ocean? Let us take a brief outlook on both the strategies as in fact India is on her way to executing both.

Should India Prioritise Deterrence by Denial Strategy in the Indian Ocean?

Some analysts argued that India should go for an offensive dealing with China in the Indian Ocean against the backdrop of the Ladakh Standoff that happened last year. But it will be illogical and imprudent to go for offensive tactics in the Indian Ocean because it can lead to blowback. Thus, India needs to adopt a sea denial strategy which proves effective in the current situation where the nation receives more conventional and sub-conventional conflicts rather than full-scale wars. The idea of taking the fight into the Indian Ocean is far from ideal. As both the nations are home to the world's largest armies it would potentially create a disaster which in turn would blow up economies dependent on these sea trade routes.

So, using this punishment form as a means of seagoing deterrent even in peacetime is not possible for India right now.

But the concept of sea denial is opaque given the conditions happenings between India and China in the IOR. Should India impose an economic blockade of all oil tankers inbound for East Asia? Should India board Chinese research/trading vessels? Implementing these kinds of moves would be considered an act of war and lead to further higher escalations with China. Thus, India must build strategic leverage in the Indian Ocean to face the stiff ongoing competition with China. Space-based data shows that India in recent times has had more engagement with smaller island nations to maintain their hard-built diplomacy over the past decade. India enjoys an immense advantage over the Indian Ocean due to its unique position and geographical features. India must explore more of these features as a first step in forming a sea denial doctrine. India still needs to focus on more active regional islands including its own islands such as Lakshawadeep in the Arabian Sea.

Doing this can provide good institutional resistance against Chinese intentions to curb Indians by their attempts to coerce or bribe political leadership. As stated in earlier stages of this paper, India must focus to fill the gap in two areas, one to commission the INS Arighat (Second SSBN) as soon as possible including more production of the same in future. Secondly, India must expand its stock of long-range ballistic **precision missiles**. These two features when incorporated can give good signs for China to make them realise that their intentions of thwarting India in the IOR will not work anymore. India must temporarily stop investing in huge warships and the same fraction of the amount can be used to manufacture long-range missiles. Thus, adopting a sea denial strategy can lead to a good roadmap for India in the Indian Ocean.

Should India Prioritise Deterrence by Punishment in the Indian Ocean?

Analysts suggest that India should go for an offensive strategy against China in the Himalayas and not in the Indian Ocean since recent conflicts have proven that India has a stronger army while China has stronger naval forces. However, India plans to go for an offensive strike in the Indian Ocean against China, a high escalation of tension will occur and there will be retaliation carried out by China along with a threatening call for nuclear strikes. Given the conditions of economies of both the nations where that are undergoing recovery from the COVID-19 pandemic, it is unlikely that China will use nuclear attacks against India and vice versa. Thus, assuming no nuclear attacks will be used, India can go for offensive strikes given the condition that the nation would withstand retaliation and diplomatic pressures. Once again as stated earlier before going for offensive strikes India must have a fully equipped military arsenal required for its advancements. Once there if at all there was a retaliation it could not lead to war since both the nations' economies in the current decade cannot withstand full-scale wars. When adopting deterrence by punishment, India must consider the incorporation of its air force also.

It is a known fact that India's air force is superior when compared to China's People's Liberation Army Air Force (PLAAF) for many reasons. There have been various instances where the Indian Air Force (IAF) conducted military drills in the IOR. In June 2021, the IAF along with US Navy's Ronald Reagan Carrier Strike Group (CSG) kicked off two-day drills along various strategic locations in the IOR. Some of the well-known IAF assets such as Jaguar Fighters, Sukhoi-30, MKIs, Phalcon AWACS aircraft, and Netra AEW&C aircraft took part in the military drills along with Indian Navy's INS Kochi (Warship), Teg, P-81 submarines.

Conclusion

Thus, India incorporating the IAF regularly in the Indian Ocean would be the key to developing her doctrine of deterrence by punishment. India must pursue serious retaliation against China if the communist nation does not stop sending its naval forces freely into the Indian waters and carrying out research in India's Exclusive Economic Zone (EEZ) without prior permission. Seeking a definite answer, **India must prioritise deterrence by denial strategy, and it would be the best choice** because as stated earlier in the essay India is not yet ready with strong naval forces as well as a good exploration of the Indian Ocean in terms of its permanent & frequent military presence deep into the waters in IOR.

References & Endnotes

1. "Indian Ocean Facts for Kids | Geography | Map | Waterways | Seaports." Kids-World-Travel-Guide.com, 2015, www.kids-world-travel-guide.com/indian-ocean-facts.html.

2. Baruah, Darshana M., and Darshana M. Baruah. "What Is Happening in the Indian Ocean?" Carnegie Endowment for International Peace, 3 Mar. 2021, carnegieendowment.org/2021/03/03/what-is-happening-in-indian-ocean-pub-83948.

3. Gopinath, P. Krishna. "Kanhoji Angre the Undefeated Admiral, and the Island Named in His Honour." The Hindu, 8 June 2019, www.thehindu.com/society/history-and-culture/kanhoji-angre-the-undefeated-admiral-and-the-island-named-in-his-honour/article27659323.ece.

4. "Aukus: Which Countries Have Nuclear-Powered Submarines?" Hindustan Times, 17 Sept. 2021, www.hindustantimes.com/world-news/aukus-which-countries-have-nuclear-powered-submarines-101631871464236.html.

5. Medcalf, Rory. "Undersea Deterrence and Strategic Competition in the Indo-Pacific." The Strategist, 30 Apr. 2020, www.aspistrategist.org.au/undersea-deterrence-and-strategic-competition-in-the-indo-pacific/.

6. MENON (Retd), Commodore VENUGOPAL. "How Will AUKUS Pact Impact India?" Rediff, www.rediff.com/news/column/venugopal-menon-how-will-aukus-pact-impact-india/20210923.htm. Accessed 17 Oct. 2022.

7. Sutton, H. I. "5 Years of Submarine Secrecy: India's Unique Arihant Class Is Still in Hiding." Naval News, 5 May 2021, www.navalnews.com/naval-news/2021/05/5-years-of-submarine-secrecy-indias-unique-arihant-class-is-still-in-hiding/.

8. "The Coming Nuclearisation of the Indian Ocean | Lowy Institute." Www.lowyinstitute.org, www.lowyinstitute.org/the-interpreter/coming-nuclearisation-indian-ocean. Accessed 17 Oct. 2022.

9. Kutty, Sumitha, and Rajesh Basrur. "The Quad: What It Is – and What It Is Not." Thediplomat.com, 24 Mar. 2021, thediplomat.com/2021/03/the-quad-what-it-is-and-what-it-is-not/.

10. Haidar, Suhasini. "Quad | the Confluence of Four Powers and Two Seas." The Hindu, 25 July 2020, www.thehindu.com/news/international/quad-the-confluence-of-four-powers-and-two-seas/article32192770.ece.

11. "Colombo Security Conclave: A New Minilateral for the Indian Ocean?" Thediplomat.com, thediplomat.com/2021/08/colombo-security-conclave-a-new-minilateral-for-the-indian-ocean/.

12. Panda, Ankit. "Report: Indian Navy Ejected Chinese Research Ship from Indian Exclusive Economic Zone." Thediplomat.com, thediplomat.com/2019/12/report-indian-navy-ejected-chinese-research-ship-from-indian-exclusive-economic-zone/.

13. White, Joshua. EXECUTIVE SUMMARY. 2020.

14. Textor, C. "China: Share of Global Gross Domestic Product 2012-2024 | Statista." Statista, Statista, 2012, www.statista.com/statistics/270439/chinas-share-of-global-gross-domestic-product-gdp/.

15. Mazarr, Michael. Perspective Understanding Deterrence. 2018, www.rand.org/content/dam/rand/pubs/perspectives/PE200/PE295/RAND_PE295.pdf.

16. "India Should Prioritise a Denial Strategy in the Indian Ocean | Lowy Institute." Www.lowyinstitute.org, www.lowyinstitute.org/the-interpreter/india-should-prioritise-denial-strategy-indian-ocean. Accessed 17 Oct. 2022.

17. Singh, Ameya Pratap. "Why India Should Pursue Deterrence by Punishment in the High Himalayas." ORF, www.orfonline.org/expert-speak/why-india-should-pursue-deterrence-by-punishment-in-the-high-himalayas-68558/. Accessed 17 Oct. 2022.

18. Bahadur (retd), AVM Manmohan. "IAF Is Key to India's 'Deterrence by Punishment' Plan against China. Now to Wait for Winter." ThePrint, 3 Sept. 2020, theprint.in/opinion/iaf-key-to-indias-deterrence-by-punishment-plan-against-china/494600/.

CHAPTER IV

India's Foreign and Security Policy

Image Credit: The Diplomatist

India is widely viewed as a rising power that will have an increasing impact on the course of international politics. What are the wellsprings of Indian policy toward the external world? How does the tension between ideational and material factors play out in the making of the world around them? This chapter deals with the elements of history, theory, and policy surrounding India. The strategic landscape shifts from the global to the Asian and thereon to the subcontinental. The essays under this chapter develops key aspects of India's external security and to develop in-depth analysis of policy world.

• • •

Convergences and Divergences in India-China Relations

(The following article is a special feature written by the guest contributor exclusively for this publication)

- Binita Verma

"China is our largest neighbour, and India's neighbourhood occupies a special place in my national development plan and foreign policy. Today, we are the world's two most populous countries and its two largest emerging economies. We are both undergoing economic transformation on an unprecedented scale and speed"

- Statement by the Prime Minister of India during the visit of President Xi Jinping of China to India" September 18' 2014.

"Both India and China are in the midst of rapid transformation. The development agenda has taken centre-stage in both our societies. Our system is different, but people in both countries are united in their aspiration for a better future. When countries of the size of China and India, together accounting for 2.5 billion people begin to unshackle their creative energies, it impacts on the whole world. The world knows it and is watching with interest. Therefore, I would like to use this opportunity to speak to you on India's development experience and on what I see a special opportunity for India and China to work together in the twenty-first century."

- Prime Minister Manmohan Singh, November 23' 2009.

Image Credit: The Quint

The relation of India and China is continued to evolve by assertions of common experience, declarations of affability and common resolution diluted and constrained by mutual suspicion and intractable problems. The rivalry also exist which hinders the cooperation and rhetoric proclaiming that the region is big enough to accommodate the simultaneous rise of both the ambitious and huge nations in their development. In 1950, India became the first country of non-socialist bloc to build a diplomatic relation with the Peoples' Republic of China and after four years, India's first Prime Minister Jawaharlal Nehru visited China in October 1954 with the agreement on 'panch sheel', the main five principles of coexistence and in 1962 they came face to face across their unsettled border in the Himalayas. As they have an ancient civilisation past, both India and China coexisted in peace and harmony for centuries. This relationship from then onwards remains volatile and ridden with tensions and frictions.

High Level Visits and Bi-Lateral Relations

In the late 1940s, there is newly independent India and an emerging Communist China were by far the two major largest countries of Third World. Apart from geographical connect, both of them could look back on the long history and a very rich civilisation and they both intended leading roles for themselves in the new developing world. Prime Minister Jawaharlal Nehru rapidly became the natural spokesperson of the Third World, as soon as India emerged from British rule. The outlook of the People's Republic of China (PRC) on the international relations was radically very different.

The Chinese Communist Party (CCP) had survived and also won a brutal civil war that lasted from 1927 to 1949 and the supreme leader of the party, Chairman Mao Zedong, summarised himself the CCP's claim to power as early as 1938: "Political power grows out of the barrel of a gun"; then form the years of late 1940s to the early 1960s, he stated that the international world arena was divided into two main hostile groups, the United States and the Soviet Union, parted by a vast zone which may include many capitalist, colonial and some semi-colonial countries from different parts of world, Europe, Africa and Asia. "But by the fall of 1962, he explicitly called for China to lead the Third World against American and Soviet hegemony."

When Beijing and Delhi, on April 29' 1954, signed the "Agreement between India and China on trade and commerce Between Tibet Region of China and India", which sanctioned the Chinese control of Tibet, the withdrawal of Indian troops from it and the handing over of the Indian postal and governmental infrastructure there. However, the two sides failed to agree on the precise demarcation of the Tibetan-Indian border. "On June 1954, in the wake of this agreement on Tibet, a visit by Chinese Premier Zhou to Delhi, where the two sides signed the joint statement on the five main principles of peaceful coexistence of panch sheel, which also included the respect and territorial integrity and sovereignty, non-aggression, non-interference in internal affairs, equality and mutual benefit and peaceful coexistence."

"On December 1958, Nehru refereed to the new Chinese maps, in a letter to Zhou, as pointing out that the two had discusses the border as late as 1956 and had agreed to respect the McMahon line in the eastern sector for the time being, although they both had considered it a legacy of the British imperialism and on January 1959, Zhou, in a very harsh reply rejected the portrayal of the border situation and denied that there was any implicit border agreement at all."

Prime Minister Rajiv Gandhi's landmark visit in 1988, as the India-China border conflict in 1962 was a serious setback to the ties, actually began a new phase of improvement in the bilateral relations between the two countries. In 1993, the signing of an Agreement on the maintenance of Peace and Tranquillity along the Line of Actual Control (LAC) on the India-China Border Areas during the Prime Minister Narasimha Rao's visit that reflected the rising stability and substance in the bilateral relations.

In 2003, during the Prime Minister Atal Bihari Vajpayee's visit in 2003, Indi and China signed a "Declaration on Principles for Relations and Comprehensive Cooperation" and also mutually decided to appoint the Special Representatives (SRs) to explore the structure of a boundary settlement from the political perspective. Later, in April' 2005, visit of Premier Wen Jiabao, the two sides established a Strategic and Cooperative partnership for Peace and Prosperity, and the signing of an agreement on "Political Parameters and guiding Principles", indicates the successful conclusion of the SR Talks.

On September' 2014, a total of 16 agreements were signed in several sectors that includes commerce and prade, railways, space cooperation, audio-visual coproduction, culture and establishment of industrial parks etc. When Prime Minster Narendra Modi visited China from May 14-16' 2015, both PM Modi and Premier Li addressed the opening session of the First State/provincial Leaders' Forum in Beijing. This series of meetings continues at the leadership level in 2016 and 2017, where they have focussed on research and innovation sector between the two countries.

After Narendra Modi took over as the Prime Minister of India in 2014, Xi Jinping was one of the top world leaders to visit New Delhi. India's insistence to raise the South China Sea in several multilateral forums subsequently did not help that beginning once again, the relationship facing the suspicion form Indian official and international world, media alike. In 2014, this relationship again took a sting as the Peoples' Liberation Army's troops entered two kilometres inside the Line of Actual Control in Chumar sector and the very next month, V.K. Singh said that China and India had come to a "convergence of views" om the threat of terrorism emanating from Pakistan. For time being, the situation was stable, but then again disruptions started to take place due to the China building trade routes, 'China-Pakistan Economic Corridor, with Pakistan on disputed territory of Kashmir.

On June' 2017, the troops of China began to extend an existing road southward with construction vehicles and roadbuilding equipment in Doklam, which is a territory claimed by both China and Bhutan and to stop this Indian troops with some weapons entered Doklam to stop these invasions by Chinese troops, but after some action and reactions, both India and China reached a consensus to put an end to the border stand off and agreed to disengage from the standoff in Doklam. In May 2018, the two countries agreed to coordinate their developmental programs in Afghanistan in the education, health and food security sectors. In 2019, India restated that it has no interest to join the China's "Belt and Road Initiative", as it cannot take a project that ignores concerns about its territorial integrity.

Chinese domination in the South China Sea was still continued even during the COVID-19 pandemic times. On may 2020, when the whole world is still confused and was not sure about how to handle the pandemic, the Chinese and Indian armed forces clashed in Nathu La, Sikkim, which causes 11 soldiers injured and later, this skirmish continues in Ladakh with a build-up of troops at various locations. Prime Minister Modi addressed the nation about this incident, where many deaths of our Indian brave soldiers shock the country and said that "the sacrifice made by our soldiers will not go in vain". There was public awareness in India about the boycott of the Chinese goods and Indian government banned 59 widely used mobile phones and desktop applications in response to the rising and escalating diplomatic dispute among the two countries.

Economic Cooperation

In the last few years, the Trade and Economic relationship between China and India has seen a rising growth. In 2000, the trade volume between them stood at US$ 3billion and in 2008, the bilateral trade reached at US$ 51.8 billion with China, which replaced the United States as India's largest "Goods trading partner". This bilateral trade includes the items, such as diamonds, cotton yarn, copper, iron ore and organic chemicals. According to the (January-March 2017), data released by the China's Ministry of Commerce, the Chinese investment in India were to the tune of US$73 million and cumulative Indian investment in China till March 2017, was reached to US$ 705million (MEA, Govt of India, 2017). The military conflict among the two nations, affect the trade sector, as many Indians did not buy 'Made in China' products, especially since the Galwan clash.

Cultural Collaboration

Both India and China are two of the world's oldest civilisations, individually they have a resiliency that has enabled them to prosper and survive through many ages and against every odd. From past thousands of years, every one of the Asian countries, as some are situated on the continental landmass, other are being islands off the mainland of Asia, has at some point been directly or indirectly influenced by one or both of these two civilisations.

There are many similarities among them and one of the most important one is their rich strategic traditions, as both of them Sunzi's (Sun Tzu's) Sunzi bingfa (The Art of War) and Kautilya's 'Arthashastra', a treatise on diplomacy, statecraft, war and empire building, were written over two thousand years agon in China and India, respectively. "The traditional Chinese concept of international relations was based on concentric circles from the imperial capital outward through variously dependent states to the barbarians. It bears remarkable resemblance to the Indian concept of mandala, or circles, as outlined in Arthashastra, which postulated that a king's neighbour is his natural ally. The Chinese dynasties followed a similar policy of encircling and attacking nearby neighbours and also maintaining friendly relations with more distant kingdoms (yuan jiao jin gong). Much like imperial China, tribute, homage, subservience-but not annexation-were the rightful fruits of victory in ancient India" (Zhong 2009).

The political relation between ancient India and China were very few and fae between. In the cultural aspect, it was always a one-sided effort, from India to China. The Buddhist and Hindu religious and cultural influence spread to China through Central Asia, and also the scholars of China were sent to the universities of India at 'Taxilla' and 'Nalanda'. During first, second and third centuries A.D. there were several Buddhist pilgrims and scholars travelled to China on the historic "silk route". As the Indian and Chinese civilizations reacted to one another during the first few centuries of Christian era, the process of religious-cultural interaction ceased after the tenth century CE (coinciding with the Islamic invasions of India) and since that time, both the countries lived as if they were unaware to each other's presence for over a thousand years, until about the beginning of the nineteenth century, when both came under the influence of European powers.

The historical civilisational interaction between India and China, "India had constructed a Buddhist temple in Luoyang, Henan Province, inside the White Horse Temple complex, which was said to have been built in honour of the Indian monks Kashyapa Matanga and Dharmaratna and the temple was inaugurated in May 2010 by the then President Pratibha Patil during her visit to China, and other than this, in February 2007, the Xuanzang memorial was also inaugurated at Nalanda. In June 2008, joint stamps were released, one stamp depicting the Mahabodhi temple at Bodhgaya and the other depicting the White Horse temple at Luoyang" (MEA, Government of India, 2017). From last few years, Yoga is becoming more popular in China and China was one of the cosponsors to the UN resolution designating 'June 21' as the International Day of Yoga.

Educational Relations

In 2006, when India and China signed Educational Exchange programme (EEP), which was an umbrella agreement for educational cooperation among the two countries and in this agreement government scholarships are awarded to around 25 students, by both the sides, in recognized institutions of higher learning in each other's country. On May 15' 2015, during the visit of Prime Minister Sh. Narendra Modi to Chinese province, both the countries signed a fresh EEP, which is the same that provides for enhanced cooperation between the institutions in the fields of vocational education and the collaboration between institutes of higher learning, etc. 25 Chinese students have been selected to join the Hindi language course for the academic year of 2017-18 under EEP scholarship awarded by Indian Council for Cultural Relation (ICCR). The students of China are also annually awarded the scholarships to study Hindi at the "Kendriya Hindi Sansthan", Agra to learn Hindi and for the year 2017-18, five Chinese students have been selected to study in Agra under this scheme (MEA, Government of India, 2017). This close collaboration in education sector among the two sides has resulted in an increase in the number of the students of Indian origin in China.

The Embassy of India maintain a decent regular communication with the MoE in China and also in universities, where there are large number of Indian origin students and in addition, officials of Embassy also visit the universities to not only build direct contact with the university authorities but also to interact with the Indian students. The students are encouraged to approach the Embassy in case they face with some kind of serious problems. This governmental approach will make sure that every student in China from Indian origin will not feel isolated and will reach out to the Embassy with no external problems.

Emerging Trends

The United States and Russia have been a consistent part of the developments in Indian and Chinese relations. Japan has also been a part of China-India relations with initiatives such as the "Quadrilateral Security Dialogue". China and Pakistan share a healthy relation that drive Chinese infrastructure projects in the disputed territory of the northern Kashmir. Both India and China engage as well as compete in places such as the Middle East, Latin America and Africa. The Middle East is very crucial to both the countries in terms of their energy security and in Africa, both seem to be mostly engaged across a wide variety of issues from developmental programmes to peacekeeping efforts. In South Asia and South-East Asia, a power balance struggle between China and India is seen in triangular relations.

Conclusion

The strategic cultures of India and China requires both to regain the power and status their leaders considering appropriate to the size, geographical location, population and historical heritage to their countries. There have been plentiful of occasions in the past, when India and China were concurrently weak and there have been some moments of cultural blossoming. The emergence of both India and China as the big economic giants, which will throw a huge new weight onto the geopolitical balance of the world. The new economic prosperity and at the same time military strength is reawakening national pride in India, which may bring some clash with the nationalism of China. The existence of two major economically powerful countries may create new tensions as they both may strive to stamp their authority on the region. In the twenty first century, the most important is the resource scarcity, which has now added a maritime dimension to the traditional Sino-Indian geopolitical rivalry.

As they are competitors for power and influence in Asia, India and China also shares interests in maintain regional stability, maintaining access to energy sources and markets, developing regional cooperation and exploiting economic opportunities. For cooperation, they have economic, environmental and cultural issues than to collide.

References & Endnotes

1. Ministry of External Affairs, Governemnt of India, "Press Statement by Prime Minister during the visit of President XI Jinping of China to India", September 18' 2014 URL: http://bitly.ws/vzvN

2. Ministry of external Affairs, Government of India, "Speech by Prime Minister Dr. manmohan Signh at the Chinese Academy of Social Sciences, Beijing", January 15' 2008 URL: http://bitly.ws/vzvQ

3. Mao Zedong, "Problems of War and Startegy," November 6' 1938, Selected Works of Mao Tse-tung, vol. 2 (Beijing Foreign Languages Press, 1967), 219-235.

4. "Communication of the Main Points of the 6th All-Country Foreign Affairs Conference", Jiangsu Shang Dang' anguan (Jiangsu Provincial Archives), 3124, zhang 145, 2-13.

5. New China News Agency, "Agreement between India and China on Trade and Intercourse Between Tibet Region of China and India", April 29' 1954, Harold C. Hinton, ed., The People's Republic of China, 1949-

1979: A Documentary Survey, vol.1, 1949-1957 (Wilmington: Scholarly Resources, 1980), 165-166.

6. "Text of Statement by Chou and Nehru", NYT, June 29' 1954.

7. Srinath Raghavan, "War and Peace in Modern India", (Houndmills: Palgrave Macmillan, 2010), pp 242, 246.

8. Bajpai, K. Selina, H. and Majari, C. eds. (2020), Routledge Handbook of China-India Relations, Routledge.

9. Chellany, B. (2012), "Rising Powers, Rising Tensions: The Troubled China-India Relationship", SAIS Review, pp.99-108.

10. Fingar, T. (2016), "The New Great Game", Stanford University Press.

11. Garver, J. W. (2001), Protracted contest: Sino-Indian rivalry in the twentieth century. Seattle: University of Washington Press.

12. Gokhale, V. (2021), "The road from Galwan: the future of India-China Relations", Carnegie India.

13. Hoffmann, S.A. (1990), "India and China crisis, Berkeley and Los Angeles: University of California Press.

14. Hongyu, W. (1995), "Sino-Indian Relations: Present and Future", Asian Survey, Vol 35.

15. Kondapalli, S. (2022), "India-China Relations", in Forging New Partnerships, Breaching New Frontiers: India's Diplomacy during the UPA Rule 2004-2012.

16. K.M. Panikkar (1957), "India and China. A study of cultural relations", Asia Pub. House: Bomaby.

(All the opinions and views expressed in this article are those of the guest contributor. It does not reflect the position of the publisher or the author)

About the Guest Contributor

Binita Verma is a Ph.D. Scholar of American Studies Program at Jawaharlal Nehru University (JNU). She is currently working on "American and Russian Policies towards the Geopolitics of the Arctic Region" as her Ph.D. topic. She did her M.Phil from the same department on "US Policy and Perspectives towards Arctic". She has completed her Masters in Politics (with specialisation in International Relations) from JNU. She has published articles on topics related to Artic Region, US-China, Geopolitics of Arctic and Indo Pacific related events. Her primary interests include to US' foreign policy, international geopolitical developments, India in Arctic and Russia-

China-US relations.

• • •

Examining India's Stance on the Rohingya Crisis

Image Credit: Sky News

When a nation feels that it is threatened by outside forces paving way for incursions into its sphere of influence, that nation will undertake any means to stop it. Myanmar, being predominantly a Buddhist nation felt that Rohingyas (a Muslim community) have started occupying their sphere of influence resulting in a decrease and freedom of the Buddhist community. For several decades, the issue of Rohingyas as a classic example of ethnic genocide exists in the books of the refugee crisis.

The Southeast Asian Buddhist nation shares borders with India, China, Thailand, Laos, and Bangladesh whose diverse population include Buddhists, Hindus, Chinese atheist government and Muslims have resulted in an international outcry for both helping Rohingyas and as well as ditching them. This paper attempts to examine India's stance on the Rohingyas crisis which is divided into three-phase stages.

The Rohingyas are a Muslim minority group who claim their native to be Myanmar's Rakhine state. However, the Myanmar government's verdict on Rohingyas stated them as undocumented immigrants originating from Bangladesh. According to Human Rights Watch, the Rohingyas are denied Myanmar citizenship, and fundamental rights such as freedom of speech, movement, and employment including land ownership in the Rakhine State.

Although stateless, they represent the largest Muslim population in Myanmar. As of 2017 nearly 1 million Rohingyas were either displaced or began to flee from the Rakhine state to Bangladesh, India, Pakistan, and Malaysia. The recent military coup that occurred last year disposed of National League for Democracy (NLD) by Tatmadaw (Myanmar's military) made the situation even worse for the Rohingyas. Many scholars have argued that an unstable political system in Myanmar has been a major contributing factor to this unsolved crisis since the 1970s.

Examining India's Stance on the Rohingya Crisis

It is a common notion for Indians to lend their hands to the helpless. From the monarchial period, India has long record of understanding stateless people and taking them inside their country by granting refugee status. The most famous Buddhist leader Dalai Lama was also given political asylum status by the past Indian government and tolerated his Tibet government in exile which he set up in Dharamshala, Himachal Pradesh.

India and Myanmar share diplomatic ties tracing back to historical, religious, and cultural dimensions. India and Myanmar signed a treaty in 1951 known as the 'treaty of friendship'. The visit of late prime minister Rajiv Gandhi to Myanmar in 1987 further strengthened the diplomatic relations between India and Myanmar. India has several ongoing economic projects (including the Rakhine state) and trade activities with Myanmar. Refugee crisis can be disastrous if not managed properly. That is the reason, India needs to equip itself with refugee management tactics while taking care not to corrupt the good bilateral relations with Myanmar. India is forced to act on the Rohingya issue due to its power projection status in Asia and the rest of the world.

First Phase

India's response to the Rohingya crisis started back in 2012 when violent conflicts erupted between Myanmar's government and Rohingyas in the Rakhine state. India intervened in the conflict, but its support was mediated more towards Myanmar. Salman Kurshid, the then external affairs minister visited Myanmar's Rakhine state to inspect the ground situation and later announced US$ one million as humanitarian aid to the Rohingyas. Later that same year current UN Secretary-General (the then UN high commissioner for refugees) Sir Antonio Guterres visited India leaving a token of appreciation for its long-standing tradition of understanding and helping refugees. Antonio on behalf of the UNHCR and New Delhi policymakers sat for a discussion about finding a solution to the Rohingya crisis. India by that time had already allowed a few thousands of Rohingyas to enter the country and settle down in Jammu & Kashmir.

The Rohingya issue started burning at an alarming rate in 2015 when Myanmar's neighbouring states such as Thailand, Indonesia and distant state Malaysia turned down permission for the boats carrying the Rohingyas to enter their territories. Several communities across the world made outcries towards India for lending her hand to Rohingya Muslims. By that time India saw a shift in power at the central level (from Congress to BJP). This led to India dealing with the Rohingya situation very differently.

India's reply to the crisis can be divided into three stages. The first stage occurred from 2012 to 2015, where one can see events of India mediating its support between Rohingya Muslims and Myanmar's government. India's approach to the crisis was shaped by a combination of factors such as geopolitical, economic, and security interests. India's actions of opening its borders to Rohingya between 2012 and 2015 were a result of gaining an international image and sustaining its governance leadership position at the regional level.

India forecasted the threats to its diversified economic projects in the Northeast region further stretching to Myanmar via the Rakhine state. India felt that any deviation in its support against Rohingya Muslims during the early phase would result in turbulences in achieving its economic objectives. India through its state-owned oil company ONGC invested nearly US$ 121 million in Shwe gas fields to draw energy supplies to meet the country's growing oil demand. The Shwe energy project was located offshore from Myanmar's disputed Rakhine state. Another concern for India was that if the nation mediated towards Rohingyas then its ambitious plan to build a road connectivity corridor from North-East India to

Myanmar would have adverse effects on its progress. India further planned to enhance the corridor with the development of port Sittwe and an in-land waterway in the Kalandan River.

In 2014, India and Myanmar Myanmar authorities signed a Memorandum of Understanding (MoU) regarding border crisis management. The growing violence against Rohingyas in Myanmar made them migrate to Bangladesh and later into India. Most of these immigrants began crossing the borders illegally. This made a loophole for terrorism activities such as illegal cross-border smuggling to grow rapidly. The MoU between the two nations provided a framework for security cooperation and intelligence sharing to strengthen their respective borders. The framework included details such as intelligence sharing on subjects related to insurgency, undocumented immigrant crossing, wildlife, arms, and drug trafficking. Both the nations agreed to help Rohingya Muslims who were deserted on borders towards safety shelters.

The then United Progressive Alliance (UPA) comprising Congress at the central level promoted the staying of Rohingyas in India without any hassle. In fact, all the events that occurred positively in the first phase of India's response to the Rohingya crisis back in 2012 were due to the decision of the Congress government. The UPA government had a mutual agreement with the state government of Uttar Pradesh to accommodate thousands of Rohingya Muslims in their lands belonging to the local government. Under the regime of Prime Minister Manmohan Singh, the Rohingyas were considered refugees and given better employment opportunities, regular donations, and identity cards from UNHCR which granted them additional humanitarian assistance from several international organisations. They were enabled to cross the borders without being questioned by the border police.

Now the question arises as to why India allowed a lot of Rohingyas to stay inside the country during the period of 2012 to 2015. It was due to a lot of money in form of donations that began to flow inside the country under the Congress regime. Once Rohingyas entered Indian territory, the then government accepted them and granted them refugee status to receive a huge sum of funds from UNHCR and several other international organisations who were ready to support them. The next question is do those funds reach Rohingyas? What did the government do?

While some funds were indeed used to uplift the welfare status of Rohingyas, most of the incoming funds fell into the hands of politicians or

NGOs who focus on refugee welfare. Hyderabad, the capital of Telangana's state is also home to 4000 Rohingya Muslims. There have been recorded incidents stating refugees from camps were detained on several charges such as forgery, cheating, criminal breach of trust, and online money swindles. These collected funds through an online campaign never reached other refugees but were instead used for living lavish lifestyles by the few culprits from Hyderabad camps. While Rohingya's small offences came into light, politically backed up money transfer labelled as Rohingya humanitarian assistance is shredded into secrecy.

Second Phase

The response to the Rohingya crisis took a different turn when BJP led central government came to power. Their agenda was fully focused on strengthening India's national security both internally and externally, so as a result, their outlook on the Rohingya crisis was different from UPA led government which supported Rohingya and delivered a huge sum of humanitarian aid when the ex-external affairs minister Salman Kurshid visited Myanmar. The first phase of response was heavily influenced by geopolitics and economic interests apart from UPA's agenda. From mid-2015 to late 2016 there was no major progression in events stating India's actions towards the Rohingya crisis as they were busy setting up the big actions which are felt in India today. The second phase started in late 2017 as a violent clash erupted in the Rakhine state between Myanmar's military and Rohingyas backed by Arakan Rohingya Salvation Army which led to 1 million Rohingyas displaced. Once again there were large incoming groups of that community into various parts of northeast India. The authorities found that large numbers (estimated to be forty thousands) of Rohingyas were undocumented while only sixteen thousands were holding government-issued refugee registered cards.

There were numerous court cases including a supreme court hearing on illegally occupied land by Rohingyas in Uttar Pradesh and various parts of Delhi, including the most important case of whether granting refugee status to Rohingyas would be justified. The last hearing by the Supreme Court of India which took place on 8th April 2021 declared that Rohingyas were standing against India's commitment to strengthen national security. Indian Government previously declared that Rohingyas are undocumented immigrants and those unregistered will be deported back to Myanmar. Soon after the deportation order was declared by India against Rohingyas, ARSA (the armed wing of that community) narrated a simultaneous serial blast bombing on an Indian Army camp in Jammu & Kashmir and Myanmar's military outpost in Rakhine state.

India's one-sided position was clearly visible when Prime Minister Narendra Modi visited Myanmar to issue a joint statement condemning the terrorist attacks which remained silent on Rohingya crisis. This ended when India re-calibrated its position to Bangladesh's proposal on helping them as they were suffocated with lot of incoming Rohingyas. Further West Bengal's local government appeal to central leadership also boosted India to re-calibrate its position to lend its support towards Bangladesh. In late 2017 India launched operation codenamed 'Insaniyat' whereby BJP led central power provided numerous humanitarian aids in cash and kind. The government stated that it helped strengthen diplomatic relations with Bangladesh. Behind the curtains India had deployed a tactical move where it aimed to seek the help of Bangladesh to deport illegal Bangladeshi immigrants from various north-eastern parts of India. Here one can note the sudden action of affection towards Bangladesh by India was a result of ending the longstanding Bangladeshi immigrant crisis in India with that longstanding Rohingya influx in Bangladesh.

In the second phase, much of the actions by India focused on the deportation of existing and incoming Rohingyas, taking a stiff stance on maintaining constant bilateral relations with Myanmar due to China card, and discarding practices of previous (UPA) government's treatment towards the Rohingyas. Much of these actions are justified by the current government as past blunders and Rohingyas are standing hindrances towards India's present agenda.

Third Phase

New Delhi started to grow concerns in late 2018 over Myanmar's enhancing diplomatic ties with the quasi-democratic government of China under the leadership of President Xi-Jinping. Chinese premier Li Keqiang issued a message to Myanmar's then-democratic leader Aung San Suu Kyi that China will help them to solve the Rohingya crisis and reinstate stability over the region of the Rakhine state. China began to back up Myanmar's 2017 counter-insurgency operations over (innocent) Rohingya Muslims claiming that they were targeting only militants.

China being a permanent member of the UN Security Council backing up this issue in the International Court of Justice would be devastating for India. Beijing proposed a three-step solution to address Myanmar's longstanding unsolved crisis. China stated that first Myanmar would implement a ceasefire followed by bilateral talks with Bangladesh mediated by Chinese policymakers paving the way towards the ultimatum of deploying repatriation treaties.

India soon after hearing Beijing's three-step solution, began to work on some tactical fire moves. New Delhi entered the third phase where it started to jolt down a long-term strategy for the Rohingya crisis and at the same time achieve its agenda. Policymakers in New Delhi realised that delaying the situation would further worsen the situation because other countries such as the United States or China would use the Rohingya crisis as leverage to achieve their geopolitical objectives. The then foreign secretary (now external affairs minister) S. Jaishankar visited the Buddhist nation in December 2017 and signed an agreement on Rakhine State Development Programme with Myanmar's Ministry of Social Welfare, Resettlement, and Relief aimed at developing the economic, social, and environment of Rakhine state to meet the needs of stateless Rohingya Muslims. The project fabricated every needs of returning Rohingya immigrants from India and Bangladesh.

The project signed under MoU was for a period of five years with funding estimated at US$ twenty-five million. The then External Affairs Minister Sushma Swaraj visited Myanmar in May 2018 to deliver a message on Rohingya's safe return to Myanmar and border crisis management. Additionally, seven MoUs were signed which focused on the development of the Rakhine state, the Joint Ceasefire Monitoring Committee, and proper management regarding the repatriation of Rohingyas back into Myanmar. According to Myanmar Times, India during the same period joined the UNSC delegation along with China, Thailand, Laos and fifteen other countries to talk subject matter regarding the humanitarian crisis in Rakhine laying further emphasis on finding a long-term solution.

Further to tackle the Chinese strong economic influence over Myanmar, India invested an additional US$ 722 Million in March 2019 to secure its economic interests in Shwe Gas Fields which is located off the coast of Rakhine state. Despite huge investments, India failed to gain supplies from Shwe but instead succeeded in countering Chinese influence over Nepal, Bangladesh, Thailand, and Myanmar.

In both phases, India had some advantages as well as disadvantages. While one can argue that India had progressively improved in its response to the Rohingya crisis during the first phase and later put down during the second phase, it is important to note that the shift in India's central government power during 2015 had introducing different agenda which is applicable for Rohingya crisis also. It can be also put in other words that if UPA led government had continued to stay in power then Rohingya welfare would have certainly improved to an extent but at the same time, India would have received a severe blow to its national security. The above-mentioned example of ARSA-led attacks on military outposts in Jammu & Kashmir is linked to terrorism. The Rohingyas are prone to Islamic radicalisation, another longstanding threat to India in Jammu & Kashmir region. Investigations carried over by the Indian Army suggested that Pakistan-based terror organisations took advantage of Rohingya camps in the Kashmir region to flush out their militant Islamic ideologies aimed at destroying religious harmony in India. Intaking a huge population of Rohingyas would pave way for militant Islamic radicalisation breeding grounds. Since 2013 several violent disturbances across the Kashmir region are either directly or indirectly related to Rohingya Muslims backed up by ARSA and Pakistan-based terror groups. To tackle the longstanding terror threats BJP led central government is forgoing the Rohingya crisis and instead making the country's national security as its priority.

Should India Reinstate a Refugee Policy and be on Course for the Rohingya Crisis?

India has been known as a refugee heaven for centuries ranging from Jews to Sri-Lankan Tamils to Tibetans except for the Rohingya case. India faced a constitutional challenge via a case called 'Mohammad Salimullah vs Union of India.' He challenged the government under article 51(c) and article 14 of the Indian Constitution which stated to honour and abide by international treaties & grant asylum to seekers, respectively. The Supreme Court ruled in favour of the government stating that under article 3 of the Foreigners Act for national security concerns, India may deport foreigners anytime if it feels so due to a security breach or whatsoever. Further India being non-signatory to the Refugee Convention, 1951 made article 51(c) invalid to be stated here. Thus, the court ruled that Rohingyas are undocumented immigrants and need to be deported back to Myanmar.

Whether India unknowingly did not sign the convention or not, it proves effective in today's scenario. India certainly will not reinstate the refugee policy nor accept inbound refugees at least for a decade or so, due to national security concerns. India has taken every measure to solve the crisis, but it ended up stagnant due to the COVID-19 pandemic and Myanmar's views on Rohingyas and the country's unstable history of frequent changes in government. Although some can argue India can proceed to solve the problem through either BIMSTEC or ASEAN, one should take note that these organisations' core agenda does not involve solving the refugee crisis. Also, these regional groupings do not possess a good track record.

This stiff stance against Rohingyas by BJP leaders has led them to fall into the hands of critics who label them as an Islamophobic and anti-Muslim political party. However, the government is still supporting registered Rohingyas whereas only undocumented people from that community are deported back to Myanmar. India is fully equipped with all the necessary policies and projects ready to solve the crisis and the only way forward lies in the fate of Myanmar's internal stabilisation. The Buddhist nationalist country holds aggressive negative sentiments against Rohingyas along with the country's unstable political system are a major contributing factor hindrance to the crisis.

One can find a precise solution when Myanmar achieves internal stabilisation.

References & Endnotes

1. Country Profile Myanmar GEOGRAPHY. www.worldvision.com.au/docs/default-source/school-resources/myanmar-country-profile.pdf?sfvrsn=0#:~:text=Myanmar%20is%20the%20largest%20country.
2. "The Rohingya Crisis." CNN, edition.cnn.com/specials/asia/rohingya#:~:text=The%20Rohingya%20are%20a%20stateless. Accessed 6 Feb. 2022.
3. "Myanmar Rohingya: What You Need to Know about the Crisis." BBC News, 23 Jan. 2020, www.bbc.com/news/world-asia-41566561#:~:text=The%20Rohingya%2C%20who%20numbered%20around.
4. "14th Dalai Lama - Life in Exile | Britannica." Www.britannica.com, www.britannica.com/biography/Dalai-Lama-14th/Life-in-

exile#:~:text=In%20the%20wake%20of%20the. Accessed 6 Feb. 2022.

5. India -Myanmar Relations. mea.gov.in/Portal/ForeignRelation/ myanmar-july- 2012.pdf. Accessed 6 Feb. 2022.

6. "Rohingya Crisis in Myanmar." Global Conflict Tracker, www.cfr.org/ global- conflict-tracker/conflict/rohingya-crisis-myanmar.

7. "India Announces $1 Million to Myanmar's Troubled Rakhine State." NDTV.com, www.ndtv.com/india-news/india-announces-1-million-to-myanmars-troubled-rakhine-state- 507565. Accessed 6 Feb. 2022.

8. Refugees, United Nations High Commissioner for. "High Commissioner Guterres Visits India, Meets Refugees." UNHCR, www.unhcr.org/news/ latest/2009/12/4b17df939/high-commissioner-guterres-visits-india-meets-refugees.html. Accessed 6 Feb. 2022.

9. Langkawi, Associated Press in. "Malaysia and Thailand Turn Away Hundreds on Migrant Boats." The Guardian, 14 May 2015, www.theguardian.com/world/2015/may/14/malaysia-turns-back-migrant-boat-with-more- than-500-aboard.

10. "India's ONGC Adds to Burma's Shwe Gas Investment | Argus Media." Www.argusmedia.com, 25 June 2020, www.argusmedia.com/en/news/ 2117589-indias-ongc-adds-to-burmas-shwe-gas-investment.

11. Karmakar, Rahul. "India-Myanmar Kaladan Project in Final Stages: Jaishankar." The Hindu, 15 Feb. 2021, www.thehindu.com/news/ national/india-myanmar-kaladan-project-in-final-stages-jaishankar/ article33844879.ece.

12. "India and Myanmar Sign Memorandum of Understanding on Border Cooperation." Www.mea.gov.in, www.mea.gov.in/press-releases.htm?dtl/23315/ India+and+Myanmar+sign+Memorandum+of+Understanding+on+B order+Cooperation. Accessed 6 Feb. 2022.

13. "Congress Gave Rohingyas Free Access to India and Land." The Sunday Guardian Live, 13 July 2019, www.sundayguardianlive.com/news/ congress-gave-rohingyas-free-access-india-land.

14. "Two Rohingya Refugees Held for 'Donation Racket' in Hyderabad." The Indian Express, 7 June 2018, indianexpress.com/article/india/two-rohingya-refugees-held-for-donation-racket-in-hyderabad-5208575/.

15. "The Rohingya Crisis, Explained: 5 Things to Know in 2020." Concern Worldwide, www.concernusa.org/story/rohingya-crisis-explained/.

16. "'Give Us Refugee Status or Deport Us to Myanmar': Rohingya Lodged in Assam Jail." Hindustan Times, 14 Dec. 2021, www.hindustantimes.com/

india-news/give-us-refugee-status-or-deport-us-to-myanmar-rohingya-lodged-in-assam-jail-101639483454871.html.

17. "International Law Omissions: Rohingya Deportation Order of the Supreme Court of India." Opinio Juris, 19 Apr. 2021, http://bitly.ws/vzwi. Accessed 7 Feb. 2022.

18. Bhattacherjee, Kallol. "We Pose No Threat to India, Says Rohingya Militant Group." The Hindu, 29 July 2018, www.thehindu.com/news/international/we-pose-no-threat-to-india-says-rohingya-militant-group/article24547191.ece.

19. "India-Myanmar Joint Statement Issued on the Occasion of the State Visit of Prime Minister of India to Myanmar (September 5-7, 2017)." Www.mea.gov.in,   www.mea.gov.in/bilateral-documents.htm?dtl/28924/
IndiaMyanmar+Joint+Statement+issued+on+the+occasion+of+the
+State+Visit+of+Prime+Minister+of+India+to+Myanmar+September+57+2017.
Accessed 7 Feb. 2022.

20. "Mamata Supports Rohingya Refugees, Sides with UN instead of PM." Hindustan Times, 15 Sept. 2017, www.hindustantimes.com/india-news/mamata-supports-rohingya-refugees-sides-with-un-instead-of-pm/story-Q8OLoUBzOzPvmVhlTmC7dM.html.

21. "Operation Insaniyat - Humanitarian Assistance to Bangladesh on Account of Influx of Refugees." http://bitly.ws/vzwm. Accessed 7 Feb. 2022.

22. "China Offers Myanmar Support over Rohingya Issue after U.S. Rebuke." Reuters, 16 Nov. 2018, www.reuters.com/article/us-asean-summit-myanmar-china- idUSKCN1NL02W.

23. "China Proposed Three-Phase Plan for Rohingya Issue." Reuters, 20 Nov. 2017,   www.reuters.com/article/us-china-myanmar-rohingya-idUSKBN1DK00I.

24. "Visit of Foreign Secretary of India to Myanmar (December 20, 2017)." Www.mea.gov.in,   www.mea.gov.in/press-releases.htm?dtl/29186/
Visit+of+Foreign+Secretary+of+India+to+Myanmar+December+20+
2017. Accessed 7 Feb. 2022.

25. "India Commits $25 Million to Develop Myanmar's Rakhine State." Hindustan Times, 21 Dec. 2017, www.hindustantimes.com/india-news/india-commits-25-million-to-develop-myanmar-s-rakhine-state/story-lpwndpPujIn1hCwBhJoqAJ.html.

26. "Visit of External Affairs Minister to Myanmar (May 10-11, 2018)." Mea.gov.in, mea.gov.in/press-releases.htm?dtl/29889/Visit_of_External_Affairs_Minister_to_Myanmar_May_1011_2018. Accessed 7 Feb. 2022.

27. "UNSC, Neighbours off to Rakhine next Week." The Myanmar Times, 26 Apr. 2018, www.mmtimes.com/news/unsc-neighbours-rakhine-next-week.html.

28. "India's ONGC Adds to Burma's Shwe Gas Investment | Argus Media." Www.argusmedia.com, 25 June 2020, www.argusmedia.com/en/news/2117589-indias-ongc-adds-to-burmas-shwe-gas-investment.

29. "Opinion | Rohingya Terrorist Group Linked to Pakistan and Militant Islamic Organizations." The Irrawaddy, 15 July 2021, www.irrawaddy.com/opinion/rohingya-terrorist-group-linked-to-pakistan-and-militant-islamic-organizations.html.

30. "India's Response to Rohingyas: A Gross Misuse of Defense of National Security and Turning Away from Its International and Constitutional Obligations." Www.jurist.org, www.jurist.org/commentary/2021/07/https-www-jurist-org-commentary-2021-07-jaiswal- kumar-rohingya-muslims-national-security-india/.

• • •

India's Diplomatic Gameplay

How successfully has India tried to manage the tensions between its strategic partnership with the United States on one hand and its strategic partnerships with Iran and Russia on the other?

Image Credit: Times of India

As the two biggest democracies of the world, India and the United States' strategic partnership began to flourish in the post-cold war era. India and the Soviet Union (now Russia) began their diplomatic engagements in 1954 to counter the US-Pakistan strategic partnership which was made through Central Treaty Organisation. In 1961, India saw a strain in its strategic partnership with the Soviet Union as India became a founding member of the Non-Aligned Movement to avoid playing the victim card due to the cold war or in other words the aggressive power-play between the US and Soviet Union. Few years ahead, the then 37th US President Nixon's decision to support Pakistan during the 1971 Indo-Pak war shut off communication between India and the US.

The dissolution of the Soviet Union in 1991 and India's foreign policy adaptation of the Unipolar World led to the development of close ties with the United States. On the other hand, upon the dissolution of the Soviet Union, now Russia retained its special strategic partnership with India. It has been termed a special and privileged strategic partnership by many scholars. India and Russia have had strong economic, military, and diplomatic relations till now. India and Russia have strong economic, military, and diplomatic engagements. India and Iran established their first diplomatic relations in 1950. India's relations with Iran suffered the same fate as the US and Soviet Union. The relationship saw a serious downfall when India became the fundamental pillar of non-Alignment cooperation while Iran openly conveyed its support for Western Bloc and enjoyed close relations with the US.

The post-cold war period once again changed the ways these four countries acted among themselves. Although India did not recognise the 1979 Islamic Revolution, the relations between the two countries began to prosper when the wind turned against the US in the context of Iran. In the post-cold War era, it can be aptly said that India had ties with US and Iran for technology, commerce, and oil trade, respectively. There are many instances where tensions began to grow between these nations due to their close diplomatic ties with other partners.

As the cold war memories have been fading away so did India's non-Alignment movement. When Narendra Modi, former chief minister of Gujarat state, was elected as Prime Minister of India in 2014, the latter statement began to make even more sense. Under the new regime, India has succeeded in a new foreign policy notion called strategic autonomy. So, what are the diplomatic tensions India is facing with the US, Iran, and Russia by adopting a strategic autonomy policy? The United States and Iran are engaged in constant odds right from the mid-1950s. During that time US was caught in the race with the UK to conquer the oil reserves of Iraq and Iran. Later the US overthrew Iran's democratic government to gain upper hand in oil reserves. Meanwhile the then imperial regime too failed shortly after leading to Iran Revolution.US cut out formal diplomatic ties it had with Iran when signing the nuclear development program under its imperial regime. In recent years US assassination of Iran's top commander Qasem Soleimani made even more anti-American sentiment stronger. Meanwhile, India having its largest oil demand satisfied by Iran has been caught in this dilemma in the US-Iran conflict.

In recent times as India seeks to balance its US and Iran ties by hunting out other sources to meet its oil demand. This move has been fuelled by the strict imposition of economic sanctions against Iran. India is carefully crafting this move as Tehran is important for New Delhi as both nations have key strategic interests in the Indo-Pacific region and condemn the

Taliban and Pakistan's action against fostering terrorism on Indian soil. India has managed to create a two-way portal in such a way that US FDI (Foreign Direct Investments) in India and India's FDIs in Iran's Chabahar port do not create hindrances. The port is vital for India in accessing major parts of Central Asia and Eastern Russia.

India has managed to send a message to Washington stating that Iran is a key element in the Indo-Pacific construct to connect Eurasia as New Delhi has plans to make it a functioning alternative to China's BRI project. Since the US has growing concerns with China regarding BRI, Washington started to show positive signs towards India's latter plan. Further India included Russia in its development project thus making these rival big powers join hands and at the same time not straining their relationship. The International North-South Transport Corridor (INSTC), currently in its beta stage aims to connect Mumbai in India to St. Petersburg in Russia via Iran.

Think tank experts have said that despite India's growing activities with Iran it will have no but noticeable impact on US-India strategic partnership.

Another potential way that India tried to dedicate the act of balancing is by engaging as a mediator in solving the US-Iran tensions. For New Delhi energy security including alternate sources of oil, will be the ultimate concern for the next few years. Non-oil trade between Iran and India stood at US$ 2.69 billion in recent years. This implies that apart from decreasing oil trade between the two countries due to US economic sanctions, New Delhi and Tehran firmly hold their strategic partnership. Scholars suggest that India maintaining relations with Iran and US in fact can be a useful bridge between Iran and the US. India with the help of international groupings such as the International Energy Agency is encouraging bilateral dialogue between US and Iran while making India source alternate energy developing infrastructure to meet its energy demands. India has been trying to indulge Washington to find value in considering new economic partnerships with Iran, rather than pushing to curb these ties.

The next irritant which is openly visible is the strategic partnership maintained between both the US and Russia by India. During the Cold War era, both countries had aggressive power-play to heighten their sphere of Influence. Although India founded the non-Aligned movement it had close military ties with the Soviet Union (now Russia). Upon dissolution after Cold War India's foreign policy adopted a Unipolar world thus retaining diplomatic ties with Russia while blooming new ties with the US. This caused much turmoil in India as it progressed towards establishing itself as a regional power in Asia.

India's abstention from the vote at the recent UNSC meeting proved that the democratic power would continue to maintain diplomatic ties with the US and Russia while guarding its interests. India attempted to balance its criticism of aligning itself too much with Russia by breaking its silence on the tensions prevailing in Europe through peaceful resolution keeping in its drafts the interests of all the parties being involved. Later a US official released a statement saying that its diplomatic ties with India have not been affected by its very own ongoing tensions with Russia. This statement proves that India is so far quite good in managing its relations with both countries.

Despite several diplomatic interventions between the US and Russia, Ukraine tensions are still in a stalemate. The US has called for strikes directly on Russia if the communist country launched any invasion of Ukraine. With regards to this context, India if it mediated towards any one country it could cost its relations with the other. So far India has taken a neutral stance against Russia-US tensions over Ukraine. India has given its statement that its relationship with US and Russia would not narrate its foreign policy, nor the countries act towards Ukraine conflict. India being a trustworthy partner of Russia for more than five decades, has begun to degrade due to India's increasing mediation towards the US which in turn made Moscow bloom its ties with Beijing. This formed a paradoxical debate among government and think tanks in India that whether Russia might be able to balance its ties with China.

During these changing dynamics of geopolitical equations, India hosted the Indo-Russian bilateral summit in December 2021 where India's Prime Minister Narendra Modi and Russian President Putin sat for a roundtable conference. Amid growing tensions both the countries also hosted their first two plus two ministerial dialogues in the same month indicating India's stronghold towards Russia as it has towards QUAD.

India to counterbalance, the nation stroked a deal earlier with the US for S-400 defence missile systems followed by a fresh deal worth US$ 100 million to produce a million units of Russian-made assault rifles. India stabilised its statements declaring that the country is prioritising its interests when pursuing the Indo-Pacific strategy while Russia strongly opposed it by saying India implemented a US-led strategy. India in recent times has channelised its resources towards Indo-Russia trade cooperation as mentioned earlier.

On a political basis, both Russia and the US possessing veto powers in the UN request India to become a permanent member of the UN security council including entry into the Nuclear Suppliers Group. In conclusion, India's pursuit of becoming global power will further make its strategic partnership with the US and Russia even more paramount, nevertheless till now India has a quite good record in maintaining strategic ties with the US, Iran, and Russia despite tensions.

• • •

India-China Rivalry from a Perspective of Security Dilemma

Would you agree that the India-China rivalry is best explained by the concept of "security dilemma"?

Image Credit: The Japan Times

India and China, the two biggest populated countries in Asia with different ideologies, cultures, and government bodies have constantly engaged in wars, tensions, and conflicts with each other at either the

Himalayan border or the Indian Ocean. Many scholars have cited the India-China rivalry as a classic example justified by the concept of the security dilemma. First, the root cause of rivalry is the characteristics of these two Asian giants. India is predominantly filled with diversified cultures and religions while China officially practices state atheism. Secondly, India is an ideologically democratic nation while China adopted communism characterised by a totalitarian dictatorship. Most importantly these two distinct nations are immediate neighbours to one another.

Now, what causes the rise, escalation, of relation to rivalry? Scholars argue that territorial disputes are major reasons between states to cultivate rivalry. India and China rising in their governance leadership in Asia and the rest of the world sees each other as antagonists. The rivalry can also happen due to nations' commitment to third parties such as signing off a security treaty or alliance thus getting dragged into a security dilemma automatically with opposite parties. The above-mentioned factors have played a vital role in shaping the Indo-China rivalry over the past decades. Although the territorial disputes started since the independence of these two countries, the rivalry started back in the 1960s.

Scholars have found three evident items in the India-China relationship over the past seven decades: hard balancing, soft balancing, and limited hard balancing. These strategies are used both by Indian and Chinese elites to constrain and curb the power of an adversary to maintain their relationship within the status quo. Scholars argue that balancing acts within rivalry nations is conditioned on a threat basis and not exclusively to increase in material capabilities. Thus, when practically applied India and China suffer from security dilemma problems, especially in areas of military capabilities and territorial disputes.

Whether the India-China rivalry is justified by the aspect of security dilemma can be answered through where these nations can find the prospect of stability vs these nations' unstable environment. The initial days of diplomatic relations between India and China were established through cooperation and shared identities between the two countries. The shared themes revolved around the notion that both nations were once victims of British colonialism later achieving liberation through years of resistance. The newly formed independent China's government was first recognised by India outside of the Communist Bloc. Nehru, the then Prime Minister of independent India sent out his appreciation regarding the agenda of the Chinese Communist Party (CCP).

The slogan 'Hindi Chini Bhai Bhai' (Indians and Chinese are brothers) reached its peak during the 1955 Bandung Conference. Both the leaders of the newly formed independent developing nations received much respect as emerging countries of the third world. The territorial disputes started to appear when China annexed Tibet in 1950. The same year Nehru was advised by Indian policymakers that China's ambition will not stop with Tibet but could also arrive in India's North-eastern region too. Later Nehru denied his security advisors' allegations on China's wicked plans in one of his 1950 parliament speeches. Although China was not happy with India's decision to grant asylum to Dalai Lama, the effort was taken from the Chinese side to not escalate the tensions into military conflicts.

The Panchsheel agreement signed between India and China to peacefully solve the outstanding irritants shows that territorial disputes are important, but not enough, factors to explain the rise of persisting rivalries. Shared identities can allow countries to mitigate territorial disputes without much escalation. However, the post-1962 Sino-Indian war proved that when nations go for deploying balancing strategies for solving immediate crises such as territorial disputes, it can lead to widening attributes such as hostility and enemy identity rather than shared identities.

India's refugee status to Dalai Lama and forcing China to follow the McMahon line was the turning point in the India-China security dilemma. China denied following it by stating that no Beijing officials accepted the 1914 Shimla accord. Furthermore, China opposed the view of the McMahon line as part of British colonialism while India defended it. China felt offended and betrayed by India due to its support of British sentiment whereas, India tried to secure her borders. Nehru started growing doubts about China's real ambitions as the Communist nation under Mao Zedong began to send its revolution worldwide. The communist supporters of India took the Chinese revolution as an inspiration thereby resulting in the growing insurgency in parts of Ladakh and the Northeast. Tensions began to escalate at borders where it turned into a military conflict. Still both the countries had a chance to defend against escalating the tensions to war, but since balancing strategies were deployed, it resulted in deepining their enmity towards each other.

Image Credit: Fair Observer

Post-1962, Nehru's strategic forecast of China's threat perception was wrong, and India started to rush toward arms acquisitions. In 1962 China was in its recovery phase from the Great Leap Forward which caused considerable damage to its economy and governance. China once again could not launch a full-scale war post-1962. Maybe Nehru's decision to arms race would have been fuelled by pressure from the Indian Parliament and India's humiliating defeat in the 1962 Sino-Indian war. China's alliance with Pakistan to counterbalance the India-US entente formed a quadratic puzzle which is unsolved to date. China-backed up Pakistan's claim over POK and Aksai Chin (now COK) in exchange for regional stability in India's North-eastern part. This created much hate towards China and paved the way for today's situation prevailing in most parts of Jammu & Kashmir and Northeast India. Both the nations began to exaggerate the level of threats posed by each other post-1962.

India began forming close ties with the Soviet Union (now Russia) to counter the China-Pakistan alliance. The Soviet Union delivered frequent military aid to India and took a stiff stance against China and Pakistan's claim on Kashmir. The then USSR envoy to the UN criticised the actions of China by stating it pursued a criminal policy with expansionist aims.

India-China rivalry started becoming intense during the post-Cold War period. Both countries are involved in increasing their geopolitical competitiveness leading to intense usage of hard balancing strategies.

Globalisation paved the way for increasing common strategic goals between the two countries. Both India and China were involved in key issues such as territorial claims in Jammu & Kashmir along with Pakistan, the South China Sea, and Indian Ocean Region. India and China are the top countries to have relatively high military budgets to rapidly modernise their military arsenal. India has been constantly improvising its ground forces while China has engaged to improvise its naval capabilities. China being the 2nd largest spender on the military, aims to protect its sea capabilities as a blue water navy like that of the US Navy.

In the 21st century, China and India began to take their rivalry into the maritime dimension. The Chinese began to expand their economy by investing in neighbouring countries such as Bangladesh, Nepal, Pakistan, and Sri Lanka for seeking alternate trade routes to connect with the West. This in turn made New Delhi grow its concerns regarding China's encirclement of India in its backyard (Indian Ocean). India began to modernise its naval forces and increase its naval presence all over the Indian Ocean citing Chinese threats in its maritime boundaries. Meanwhile, most parts of the Chinese BRI project began to operate thereby giving the communist nation access to fast transit portal across the Indian Ocean. China with the context of guarding its merchant vessels against the Indian Navy started increasing its Naval presence inside the Indian Ocean.

Though nuclear dynamics played vital roles during the cold war, recent deployments of nuclear-powered submarines by China in the Indian Ocean, made New Delhi rapidly strengthen its Navy to the next level. Meanwhile, both nations are caught in a security dilemma across the Himalayan border. The recent standoffs such as Demchok, Doklam, and Ladakh have further heightened the process of infrastructure construction between both countries. The continuous hard balancing strategy from both countries would create many uncertainties in upcoming years. During the COVID-19 pandemic once again both nations were caught in serious economic backdrops.

As an ending note, I agree with the statement that India-China rivalry is best explained by the concept of the security dilemma.

CHAPTER V

Cross-Strait Relations

Relations across the Taiwan Strait are one of the most intricate, intractable, and consequential security and political questions in Asia and rest of the world. As a proverbial flashpoint, it remains an enduring source of instability or concern in regional and global affairs. The essays under this chapter will engage the readers in an in-depth examination of the issues surrounding China-Taiwan relations. The essays will explore and discuss, among other things, the theoretical facets, political history, identity politics, political economy, and security and military dynamics of cross-strait relations. The goals, strategies, and domestic underpinnings of the main actors in this ongoing and evolving political story will also be examined.

The essays were written after careful study and consideration followed by the essays which will deliver the following;

- Gain a fuller and deeper insight of the issues surrounding one of the more enduring and intransigent cases of a 'divided nation' in international politics.
- Develop a better appreciation of the nuances, grammar and complexities in cross-strait relations.
- Acquire additional knowledge and analytical expertise for a specialisation in the international relations and study of Northeast Asia.

• • •

Taiwan's Strategy to Reduce Economic Dependence on China

Introduction

Since 1949 the Republic of China (ROC) otherwise called Taiwan has been struggling to establish itself as a separate government entity. The People's Republic of China (PRC) otherwise called mainland China or simply China has vowed by making unification of Taiwan into its mainland as an agenda of national concern. Though both the countries predominantly consist of similar ethnic groups, they have diverse cultural and political views from their Communist counterpart. Taiwan has a democratically elected form of government thus, having a unique identity as an independent island nation and relations with mainland China. This unique nature also directly correlates with Taiwan's economic component.

Image Credit: Radio Free Asia

Right from the dawn of the Cross-Strait confrontation between China and Taiwan, the latter has had discriminatory policies of trade and commerce towards its counterpart. This left a serious impact not only on China and Taiwan but also on nations having trade interests in Taiwan Strait. Further free and open trade practices were hindered due to the result of regular escalating tensions between China and Taiwan. Despite (Taiwan) being an important country in the East Asian economy, the past decade has been a watershed for its economy due to reducing foreign direct investments because of bitter bilateral relations with Mainland China.

Taiwan has the least share in participating in the regional and international trade practises thereby cutting access to other economies of the world. Despite all these shortcomings, reports have suggested that Taiwan has done exceptionally well in maintaining its economy and will continue to boom higher in upcoming years. Taiwan has shown that a Chinese democracy can be governed effectively including the economic dimension. Even as the world suffered a pandemic, Taiwan grew as a high-income yielding economy for the previous year.

The Economic Cooperation Framework Agreement is a boon in Cross-Strait confrontation for Taiwan because it enabled the Chinese democracy to grab an opportunity to integrate more into the East Asian Economy and beyond. Due to the agreement Taiwan had an option to either pursue preferential trade practices with other countries or to pursue a multilateral trade strategy and focus on domestic reforms that will bring larger economic gains, and diversification and avoid political risks, especially with Mainland China sailing smoothly across Cross-Strait.

This paper aims to find out what strategies were used by Taiwan to reduce its economic dependence on China and how the same can be achieved in the forthcoming years.

Overview of Taiwan's Economy

Before we dive deep into the mainframe of the question, it is important to understand the model of Taiwan's economy. This section of the paper will find out and analyse Taiwan's economic model. It has been reported that Taiwan runs a highly developed free market economy. Taiwan's economy is reported to be the 8th largest in Asia and 18th largest in the world depending on purchasing power parity index, making the country to be included in the advanced economies group by the International Monetary Fund (IMF). The World Bank also classified Taiwan under the high-income level economies grouping

History of Taiwan's Economy

Upon probing the reports, we can find references that Taiwan has been transformed into what it is today with the help of the US. During the early 1950s to late 1960s, the US was the major financial aid donor for Taiwan and its sole foreign investor. Here it can be noted that the US on one hand has used Taiwan as a proxy to invest heavily in Mainland China. Thus, Taiwanese investment in mainland China is estimated to exceed over US\$ 150 billion. Taiwan also holds major investments share in other parts of Southeast Asia.

Historically, the country carefully crafted its strategy to minimise its dependence on mainland China, starting with industrialisation by land reforms. Taiwan's rapid democratisation and economy being open led to US investments as stated above which accounted for 30 per cent of the country's GDP during the period from the 1950s to 1960s. Along with US investments and KMT's proper planning, the country witnessed rapid advancement in industrial and agricultural aspects including people's living standards. The Chinese democracy's economy saw a shift from an agricultural economy to an industrial-based economy post-1960s. Due to this change in economic orientation, Taiwan's GDP grew by an average of 9.27 per cent each year thereafter.

The smooth sail of Taiwan under the US' care went off the tide when America established its formal diplomatic ties with mainland China by severing ties with Taiwan. Though security relations were maintained between the two sides, the commitment to financial aid and economic links were cut off. Thus, the Taiwan policymakers took a hard turn from a subsidised import economy model to an export-led growth economy model. The country's government took the opportunity to shed its agriculturally based economy to utilise the significant growth it could achieve by shifting towards the implantation of an economy run by heavy industries and infrastructure developments. The government scaled up their economic activities towards more open markets and rapidly shifted towards the privatisation of public-owned enterprises.

During the 1980s, Taiwan's government started integrating advanced electronics-based industries into its economy thus, fully shedding its cheap and labour-intensive manufacturing sectors. Post-1980s, Taiwanese investments in mainland China increased which spurred Cross-Strait trade aspects thereby decreasing the Chinese democracy's dependence on the United States. Due to the country's financial policies, Taiwan suffered little during the financial crisis from 1997 to 1999 as compared to other nations.

The nutshell of the historical economic build of Taiwan indeed shows very much less interaction with mainland China. Today mainland China stands as Taiwan's number one exports and imports partner. Somewhere down the road, China overtook America to make the Chinese democracy dependent on them. So where did the dragon's gameplay occur?

How did Taiwan became Economically Dependent on China?

It all started during the post-1990s and rapidly during the past two decades. During this period Taiwan's economy deepened its ties to its counterpart.

Today, China is Taiwan's largest trading partner absorbing nearly 30 per cent of the island's exports. Ironically, the dependence on mainland China started during the administration of Chen Shui Bian who was Taiwan's first president of the Democratic Progressive Party (DPP) whose core agenda was pioneering independence from China.

Despite advocating Taiwanese national identity, under his administration, the government raised the value of the island's exports which resulted in a total value of $66 billion at the end of his tenure in 2008. Furthermore, in 2015 exports by Taiwan accounted for 53 per cent of its GDP, whereby mainland China was the leading market for its exports. Ma Ying-jeou who took over the administration from Chen made the economic growth even more modest although the KMT leader did not deepen the economic ties between the two sides. Under Ma's leadership, the government opened the island nation for tourism to China, which lead to a rapid increase in tourists from the mainland and vice versa. Today, mainland Chinese citizens account for half of the incoming visitors to Chinese Taipei.

The economic ties between Taiwan and China now went over control. The second largest trading partner of Taiwan which is Hong Kong once again comes under China thus, indirectly swallowing the second spot too. The third largest trading partner the US does not even come closer enough to the amounts of exports and imports done between China and Taiwan including Hong Kong. Thus, deeply connected by exports and imports for revenue, Taiwan has become heavily dependent on China which developed strongly over several years. So, what are the strategies developed by Taiwan to deter reliance on China? The further section of this paper will analyse all the possible strategies constructed by Taiwan to become less reliant on mainland China.

Strategies posed by Taiwan to counter Chinese dependency

Taiwanese in China

Analysing the past few years data has shown that nearly 2 million Taiwanese people live in mainland China permanently. These people with Taiwanese links are running small and medium-scale enterprises known as Taishang, which are often employing thousands of mainland Chinese citizens in their businesses. Hon Hai Precision Industry or better known as Foxconn is the largest business that employs nearly 1 million Chinese citizens on the mainland. This led to a transfer of over $10 billion worth of FDIs from Taiwan to China in the past decade. On the other hand, a 2016 report shows that such kinds of FDI flowing from China to Taiwan remains comparatively smaller at $215 million because of strict regulations from the latter country's control over where China can invest.

Though China had strict economic controls like Taiwan, the latter nation's businessmen were successful in penetrating and navigating through the highly complicated bureaucracy. Will Taiwan's method of counter-investing in mainland China prove effective? In short, yes it has proved effective for Taiwan as revenue generated is ploughed back into the country as profits but still, it's a very dangerous way of constructing countermeasures.

The Chinese democracy's top revenue-generating sources come from the technology sector which is involved in hardware manufacturing and assembly. Furthermore, all the Taiwanese technological-based companies do business across the strait which makes them prone to political backlash and in the worst-case scenario could lead to the dissolution of the companies. It has been reported that Taiwanese companies like Taiwan Semiconductor Manufacturing Company (TMSC) and MediaTek are facing increasing competition from their respective Chinese counterparts which are mostly government-owned corporations.

In case of the Chinese government's pressure, companies like device makers could cancel their contracts with Taiwanese chip manufacturing industries thereby switching to domestic makers such as Spreadtrum or Tsinghua Unigroup. Taiwanese investments in China would be dangerous for the island nation since those companies are bound by the legal laws of China and changing dynamics of China such as economic slowdown could also, in turn, affect Taiwan leading to its economic slowdown.

<u>The Economic Cooperation Framework Agreement</u>

ECFA was signed on 29th June 2010 and is in force to date, it is indeed another significant strategy devised by Taiwan to normalise economic relations with China without creating pressures or escalating tensions including being over-dependent on China. The ECFA is significant in many dimensions like political and economic in cross-strait relations which enabled Taiwan's entry into the regional and international economic access.

The ECFA removed the restrictions and import bans of goods from mainland China to Taiwan. It also resulted in cutting down tariffs for several hundreds of categories of goods and services mostly comprising industrial components between mainland China and Taiwan. It set the foundations for negotiations and cooperation amid the escalating pressures between both countries. China has given more concessions to Taiwan than the latter itself did to its counterpart and the agreement set up cross-strait economic cooperation management panels which have been holding several regular meetings for bilateral talks on investment protection, commodity trade and services, and peaceful settlement of disputes mechanisms.

Previously the result of the ban on Chinese imports and exports to Taiwan by the island nation resulted in a low share of trade between both countries. However, the numbers were still significantly higher amounting to 16.5 per cent of total Taiwanese exports to China and 30.9 per cent in previous years. With the intervention of the World Trade Organisation (WTO), bans were lifted, and both countries resumed their imports and exports. It has been reported that Taiwan had imposed these bans under the guise of political and economic security concerns that have been rampant in the name of corrupting Taiwanese identity. Trade relations with China would pose danger for Taiwan since the dragon could force, coerce, and manoeuvre the island nation towards unification.

On the other hand, Taiwan could also gain leverage through political gains since economic integration with China may reduce the risks of tensions in cross-strait relations thereby having free bilateral trade with other countries beyond cross-strait boundaries. Many scholars in China look at the ECFA as an opportunity for the first step toward economic reunification between the mainland and Taiwan. But this necessarily does not mean that the political reunification agenda of China need not forgo the benefits reaped from ECFA. Doing so will put political constraints on the mainland due to the usage of economic coercion.

Taiwan's strategy of participating in production networks

Unlike Europe where the economy is led by an institution-based model, East Asia is often characterised by a market-led economy which applies to the Chinese democracy also. Since Taiwan was short of financial aid especially US cutting its ties with the island nation it decided to practise unilateral trade and investment liberalisation due to domestic commitments. To lessen its economic interdependency with China, Taiwan in the past decade had constantly engaged with the rest of the East Asian nations by boosting its exports which at one point of time collectively amounted to 40 per cent. The exports included machinery, transport equipment, and information technology services.

A fixed pattern of investment by Taiwanese companies can be seen in Southeast Asia in the past decade as a notion for reducing economic interdependency on China. A thing to be noted here is that these Taiwanese companies are either subsidiaries of US companies or backed up by them. Thus, the technological intensive parts are shipped from Taiwan to elsewhere countries in Southeast Asia hosting the assembly hub of production which results in an ultimate skip of China in the whole scenario. This pattern has rapidly come into force since the world has been hit by COVID-19.

Although Taiwan taking the necessary steps to curb its dependence on China by looking toward Southeast Asian nations, the outcome of the results was not fruitful due to escalating tensions between both countries in recent years.

Taiwan's Free Trade Agreement

The above-discussed ECFA paved way for Taiwan to sign more Free Trade Agreements (FTAs). Additionally, the ECFA will protect Taiwan's FTA trading partners from political backlash or discriminatory comments by China. Even by pursuing this strategy Taiwan was able to bypass Chinese economic interventions and join hands with small trading partners but missed out on other larger trading partners who primarily did trading with China. However, reports have suggested that Taiwan was able to marginalise regional integration via FTAs but once again failed to try to integrate fully into the international economic ring. It can be observed that Taiwan's economic activities are hindered product of political backlash from China which also prevented it from signing away FTAs with larger trading partners.

Due to the above complications, Taiwan has been effectively cutting itself off from fully participating in the regional economic activities, especially with ASEAN nations. Also, some other countries in the East Asia region such as Japan, Singapore, and the EU have shown immense interest in pursuing FTAs with Taiwan as the island signed ECFA past decade. Additionally, the US-backed up Taiwan's ECFA so the island nation would sign more FTAs without much concern about insecurity towards China.

The FTAs strategy is such a brainstorming move by Taiwan policymakers. Though the FTA unlocked new trading opportunities for Taiwan it failed to enable access to economic partners in its backyard. To date, the FTAs signed by Taiwan are not with any countries that have a big enough share in East Asia thereby making no huge difference. The countries with which Taiwan signed FTAs were El Salvador, Guatemala, Nicaragua, Honduras, and Peru. All those countries belong to Central America thereby giving access to potential American markets for Taiwan. But probing into the trade shares held by these countries with Taiwan accounted for less than a per cent.

Taiwan took a bifold initiative to enhance its economic diplomacy post-ECFA. Taiwan tried to sign more FTAs at any cost (one such being the US) and the other initiative is to imitate its neighbouring countries other than China. Since FTAs would put forth normalisation of Taiwan's economic relations across the strait, the Chinese democracy took its risk to approach major countries having huge trade shares as the political discrimination or backlash by China could not be that devastating. Also, on one hand, the FTA meant that commerce activities between China and Taiwan will be normalised posing no dangers so the island nation can integrate more regional vice. This on the other hand could limit Taiwan's engagement with other trading partners.

Recent Economic Development Tactics employed by Taiwan

Taiwan never changed the theme of its exports as a form of a strategic approach for ages. But its trading partners have changed from time to time. COVID-19 has been a boon in one way for Taiwan since exports and imports to and from China have drastically reduced. Due to COVID-19, as the concept of work from home and video conferencing rose to fame so did the technology's raw materials such as semiconductor chips. In the past two years, Taiwan's economy grew as the largest in Asia and performed well combined than in the previous decade which allowed the island country to tap into potential resources.

As the COVID-19 pandemic hit worse in China, the nation imposed a nationwide lockdown due to which several regional technological manufacturing hubs were halted. As a result, several technological companies turned their eyes toward Taiwan. The Chinese democracy took its biggest ever chance by grabbing this golden opportunity. The global shortage for machine components filled the Taiwanese chip makers' order books thus, making them produce the biggest output leap ever than the previous decade.

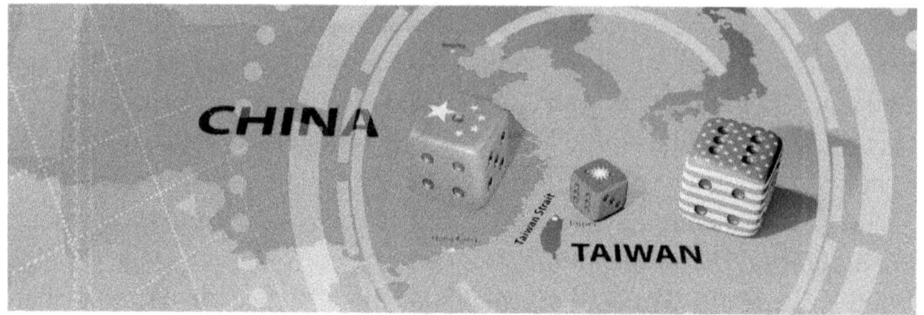

Image Credit: International Bar Association

Technology giants such as Apple, Microsoft and Google imported goods from Taiwanese-based companies resulting in them outrunning their regional peers in China. Taiwan's economy has shown a rebound of economic growth amounting to 6.1 per cent which is 12 times higher than ever recorded since the nation was swept by a financial crisis past decade. For the first time in three decades of Taiwan's export history, the nation outran its largest economic trading partner China to those other countries. Taiwan's exports to the United States amounted to 30 per cent, and Europe and Southeast Asian nations stood at 37 per cent and 32 per cent respectively while China was locked at 23 per cent of total exports.

The above resulted in the largest ever recorded of capital investment repatriation by Taiwanese countries in their homeland. The overseas Taiwan-based business brought back nearly US$ 37 billion (NT$ 1,038 billion) which was later retained as Taiwan's domestic capital investment last year. Taiwan's semiconductor industries hold a major contribution to the latter amounts. Nevertheless, reports claim that Taiwan's participation in regional trade deals is uncertain. Further Taiwan is less likely to join the Regional Comprehensive Economic Partnership due to China's heavy share of political and trade weights in the agreement. While most of the Comprehensive & Progressive Agreement for Trans-Pacific Partnership (CPTPP) members are small economies, Taiwan has more chances to join the pact and gain greater net benefits than any other member.

Analysts argue that Taiwan's greater participation in regional and international economic forums would provide an additional layer of economic security in case China ever put economic sanctions. Although the Chinese democracy's investment pattern shifts away from China in recent years to diversify its export partners, it might take a long time for Taiwan to drastically reduce its counterpart's shares in their external trade activities to achieve economic acceleration.

TS Lombard an economist at a research firm estimated that Taiwan accounted for nearly 83 per cent of global chip manufacturing production output which means the island nation would possibly attain absolute monopoly status for semiconductor industries in near future. Such an event could enable Taiwan to win over weapons deal with the United States while decreasing pressure from China. Further TS Lombard claims that soon mainland China could become dependent on Taiwan for semiconductors due to rising tensions with the US. Though the economic dependency gets reversed here from Taiwan to China, still the element of economic interdependency exists between the two nations.

If that's the case, then China will once again become the largest trading partner of Taiwan in the upcoming years thereby cutting the string of closeness between the US and Taiwan. This will also further lead to China becoming Taiwan's sole competitor in the global market. China pursues this strategy of making itself being reliant on Taiwan to keep the chain of economic interdependencies intact. TS Lombard says that as far as Taiwan keeps its export with China arguably less and focuses its expertise on the electronics sector for economic growth, job opportunities and investments the island nation would be little mediated towards the safer side.

Contradictory reports regarding the subject matter shed light on a slightly different perspective. Those reports claim that Taiwan will continue to increase its exports while demands from the US will increase bifold times. Given the context of the pandemic private consumption is unlikely to raise anytime soon which will have a direct negative adverse on Taiwanese companies. While two decades ago Taiwan's main concern was shifting the focus of its economic model to an export-based income structure, today the country must focus on confronting the challenges arising from domestic manufacturing activities.

Reports have suggested that economic integration with Taiwanese companies has slowed in China in recent years, but this will not necessarily stop the dependency altogether at once. Given the geopolitical complications and uncertainties, Taiwan must leverage the recovery phase of the COVID-19 pandemic situation to tie up with those trading partners having the highest trade shares in East Asia.

The US-Taiwan FTA

Not only trade restrictions were put up with China but also with the US. The Chinese democracy had put trade bans on pork and beef imports which greatly hindered the FTA between these countries. Secondly, the United States was more focused on Trans-Pacific Partnership (TPP) under pre-Biden administrations. Even Taiwan was not invited to the TPP by the US delegations since it would create a huge political backlash against the island nation from China.

Another hindrance which causes the US to maintain strategic ambiguity and not aggressively pursue FTA with Taiwan is due to the recognition of the 'One-China' principle by US policymakers. For three decades to secure its interests abroad, the US cut off its ties with Taiwan and recognised the PRC as one and only China. To this date, it has created a hindrance for the US to directly get involved in Taiwan's administration matters. Under the administration of Biden and Tsai, all these tides changed in a positive direction. Back in 2020, Taiwan removed the long-standing ban on pork and beef imports followed by US$ 12 billion in outbound investments towards the US last year.

US President Biden has no interest in reviving the US' TPP interests. Meanwhile, Taiwan has sought its firms to quit mainland Chinese territories and involve more in Southeast Asia through Taiwan's 'New Southbound Policy'. Since the COVID-19 hit across the world, Taiwan has restructured its economic policy frameworks in such a way that Taiwanese firms abroad must plough their profits back into the homeland. Having a huge capital in hand, Taiwan must seek to pursue FTA with the US as it will ensure the island nation's political autonomy and keep China at bay.

The United States under trump's administration witnessed growing tensions with China which paved the way for US-Taiwan FTA to occur. But signing the accord at that time of escalating tensions would put Taiwan under tremendous pressure. Given a global pandemic and change in the administration of the US, the signing of the US-Taiwan FTA does not appear to occur anywhere close. Yet growing tensions with China especially for the US would push the Biden administration to change their policy of strategic ambiguity and support Taiwan more including a gift of FTA.

Conclusion

All the strategies pursued previously by Taiwan to reduce its dependency on China yielded the exact opposite results and few tactics although took Taiwan on the road to achieving its goals and objectives it landed the country in the state of economic interdependency as China became the largest trading partner of Taiwan. This happened not only due to the US cutting off its bilateral relations with Taiwan but also by cutting off the financial and strategic aid it was providing to the nation. Another blunder mistake by the US was recognising the One-China principle which made Taiwan helpless in a broader perspective.

The above events happening post-1980s, Taiwan policymakers took a huge step to shift from an agriculturally based economy to a technology manufacturing economy using the aid obtained from the US government since the island administration saw their future potential in it. In post-1990s Taiwan became powerful as a technological production hub focusing on semiconductors which are the heart of any machine. Meanwhile, US-backed up technological companies were set up in China leading to the country's rapid modernisation. Taiwan to keep its country running while not having official recognition as a state, started to export its products to China thus, entangling towards the biggest crisis it faces today. Given the context of rapid military modernisation of China was nearly impossible for both Taiwan and the US to join hands directly in the Taiwan Strait.

Core problems between China and Taiwan are much bigger than the economic dimension; in fact, the economic realm is just a small entanglement in a larger ring. The potential solutions to solve the Cross-Strait confrontations include symbolic unification (one China), functional unification (like the EU model), loose federation (Taiwan demilitarisation), or setting up Taiwan like a Hong Kong model (Special Administrative Region- SAR). Unfortunately, none of the potential solutions will take place since Taiwan and China went out of their original agenda of Unification and Reunification. Taiwan today especially focuses on achieving an independent status quo thereby aiming at establishing a unique Taiwanese identity.

Given the COVID-19 pandemic, China had more internal problems to deal with since its international image was tarnished as the virus is said to have originated from Wuhan Lab in China. Thus, during the wink of Chinese policymakers trying to fix their internal problem, Taiwan was able to rise as Asia's largest economy putting China as its least traded partner. Now given the revival phase of the world, the Taiwanese government must focus on making the US-Taiwan FTA occur so that Taiwan would potentially put the US once again as its largest trading partner and tap into bigger trading partners internationally followed by reducing the economic dependency on China.

References & Endnotes

1. Lin, Syaru Shirley. "Taiwan's Continued Success Requires Economic Diversification of Products and Markets." Brookings, 15 Mar. 2021, www.brookings.edu/blog/order-   from-chaos/2021/03/15/taiwans-continued-success-requires-economic-diversification-of-products-and-markets/

2. "World Bank Country and Lending Groups – World Bank Data Help Desk. Web.archive.org, 11 Jan. 2018, web.archive.org/web/20180111190936/datahelpdesk.worldbank.org/knowledgebase/articles/906519#High_income/.

3. "Taiwanese Investment in China - Winkler Partners." Web.archive.org, 21 Apr. 2011, web.archive.org/web/20110421035236/www.winklerpartners.com/a/comment   taiwanese-investment-in-china.php

4. "The Story of Taiwan - Economy." Archive.org, 2009, web.archive.org/web/20100202032138/www.taiwan.com.au/Polieco/History/ROC/report04.html.

5. "Wayback   Machine."   Web.archive.org,   web.archive.org/web/20140709162957/www.aric.adb.org/pdf/aem/external/financial_market/Sound_Practices/tap_bnk.pdf. Accessed 25 May 2022.

6. "The Definition, Purposes, Functions and Services of Incubation Centers." Incubator.moeasmea.gov.tw, incubator.moeasmea.gov.tw/en/incubation-centers-en/incubation-centers-info-en. Accessed 25 May 2022.

7. 遠見天下文化出版股份有限公司. "從前登陸像成吉思汗，現在台青登陸是白骨
精 | 范榮靖 | 遠見雜誌." 遠見雜誌 - 前進的動力, www.gvm.com.tw/article/17768.
Accessed 26 May 2022.

8. Horwitz, Josh. "Charted: Taiwan's Economy Is More Dependent on China than Ever

Before, Making Trump's Threats Dangerous."Quartz, Quartz, 16 Dec. 2016, qz.com/861507/charted-taiwans-economy-is-more-dependent-on-china-than-ever- before-making-trumps-threats-dangerous/.

9. CHENG TING-FANG, Nikkei staff writer. "Mediatek Posts Record Sales but Faces Stiff Competition." Nikkei Asia, Nikkei Asia, 3 Aug. 2016, https://asia.nikkei.com/NAR/Articles/MediaTek-posts-record-sales-but-faces-stiff- competition.

10. Kastner, Scott L. "Political Conflict and Economic Interdependence across the Taiwan Strait and Beyond." Stanford University Press, Stanford University Press, 2009, www.sup.org/books/title/?id=16474.

11. Peter Drysdale & Xinpeng Xu, 2004. "Taiwan's Role in the Economic Architecture of East Asia and the Pacific," Asia Pacific Economic Papers 343, Australia-Japan Research Centre, Crawford School of Public Policy, The Australian National University.

12. By Virginia Marantidou - Pacific Forum. https://pacforum.org/wp-content/uploads/2019/02/140624_issuesinsights_vol14no7.pdf.

13. Zhao, Hong, and Sarah Tong. East Asian Policy East Asian Policy East Asian Policy
East Asian Policy East Asian Policy 69 Implications of Taiwan- Mainland Economic Cooperation Framework Agreement. research.nus.edu.sg/eai/wp-content/uploads/sites/2/2017/11/Vol1No3_ZhaoHongSarahTong.pdf. Accessed 26 May 2022.

14. Roy, Denny. (2004). Cross-Strait Economic Relations: Opportunities Outweigh Risks. 13.

15. Ando, Mitsuyo, and Fukinari Kimura. "The Formation of International Production and Distribution Networks in East Asia." National Bureau of Economic Research, 1 Dec. 2003, www.nber.org/papers/w10167.

16. Athukorala, Prema, and Nobuaki Yamashita. "Global Production Sharing and Sino–US Trade Relations." China & World Economy, vol. 17, no. 3, 2009, pp. 39–56, ideas.repec.org/a/bla/chinae/v17y2009i3p39-56.html.

17. Dent, Christopher M. "Taiwan and the New Regional Political Economy of East Asia."
The China Quarterly, vol. 182, June 2005, pp. 385–406, https://doi.org/10.1017/s030574100500024x.

18. Hoan, Truong Quang, et al. "Taiwan–ASEAN Trade Relations: Trade Structure and Trade in Value Added." China Report, vol. 55, no. 2, May 2019, pp. 102–124, doi:10.1177/0009445519834371.

19. World Trade Organization. World Trade Report Trade in Natural Resources. 2010, www.wto.org/english/res_e/booksp_e/anrep_e/world_trade_report10_e.pdf.

20. Armstrong, Shiro Patrick. "Taiwan's Asia Pacific Economic Strategies after the Economic Cooperation Framework Agreement." Journal of the Asia Pacific Economy, vol. 18, no. 1, Feb. 2013, pp. 98–114, https://doi.org/10.1080/13547860.2012.742668.

21. "Taiwan GDP Growth Fastest in Decade in 2021 on Strong Exports." Nikkei Asia, asia.nikkei.com/Economy/Taiwan-GDP-growth-fastest-in-decade-in-2021-on-strong- exports#:~:text=Taiwan. Accessed 27 May 2022.

22. " 新 聞 稿 ." Www.mof.gov.tw, www.mof.gov.tw/singlehtml/384fb3077bb349ea973e7fc6f13b6974?cntId=de888ef90 75748a7974ea40bb93349e0. Accessed 27 May 2022.

23. 國家發展委員會. "國家發展委員會." 國發會全球資訊網, 29 June 2015, www.ndc.gov.tw/Content_List.aspx?n=6C3C3045CFD283A2.

24. "Taiwan's Economy Outperforms amid COVID-19 Crisis." East Asia Forum, 31 Jan. 2022, www.eastasiaforum.org/2022/01/31/taiwans-economy-outperforms-amid-covid-19-crisis/.

25. Editor. "Challenges for Taiwan's Defence & Economic Security and Its Required Efforts to Ensuring a Sustainable Peace." Taiwan Insight, 1 June 2021, taiwaninsight.org/2021/06/01/challenges-for-taiwans-defence-economic-security-and- its-required-efforts-to-ensuring-a-sustainable-peace/.

26. Lee, Yen Nee. "Taiwan's Economy Outgrows China's for the First Time in 30 Years, as Chips Demand Soars." CNBC, 1 Feb. 2021, www.cnbc.com/2021/02/01/taiwan-economy-outgrows-china-first-time-in-decades-as-chips-demand-rises.html.

27. Kharpal, Arjun. "China Wants Its Semiconductor Industry to Catch up with the U.S. — but That Won't Be Easy." CNBC, 14 Sept. 2020, www.cnbc.com/2020/09/14/china-semiconductor-industry-tries-to-catch-up-with-us-chip-makers.html.

28. Division, US Census Bureau Foreign Trade. "Country and Product Trade Data." Www.census.gov, www.census.gov/foreign-trade/statistics/country/index.html.

29. "Taiwan's Trade Policies: Strategies and Constraints." The National Bureau of Asian Research (NBR), www.nbr.org/publication/taiwans-trade-policies-strategies-and- constraints/.

• • •

Paper/Article Review

(Review and critical analysis of an article/paper written by a subject matter expert on Cross-Strait relations)

I have chosen the paper titled "Ambiguity, Economic Interdependence, and the US Strategic Dilemma in the Taiwan Strait" written by Scott L. Kastner, published in Journal of Contemporary China (2006), 15(49), November, 651-699. The issue of Mainland China and Taiwan has been a long-standing dispute with amalgamation various problems such as land sovereignty, identity, and governance. In recent years, tensions have once again risen, leaving the US policymakers to take a tough stance between intervention and policy of strategic ambiguity. In the above-mentioned article, the writer has made critical views on US' agenda in the Taiwan Strait, thoughts on US intervention, arguments on strategic ambiguity and followed by shedding light on the US strategic dilemma in the Taiwan Strait.

In his opening remarks, Kastner has connected the roots of the US dilemma that dates to the end of Chinese Civil War in 1949. The US, seeking for more balanced diplomatic ties in the Taiwan Strait, severed its ties with Taipei to officially initiate relations with Beijing. The initial dilemma thus started in 1980 due to the long-standing defence treaty named "Sino-American Mutual Defense Treaty" where the US had agreed to defend Taiwan from invasion by Mainland China. I agree with author's remarks stating that the US began to face stiff dilemma post 1980 where rapid democratisation of Taiwan occurred.

The author has given two reasons for supporting the latter statement. First, due to the rapid democratisation of Taiwan it resulted in increased value of preserving its democratic identity for the US. Similarly, due to the Cold War effect India though being democratic followed the policy of Non-Aligned Movement (NAM) which might have resulted in US actions for choosing Taiwan card against Mainland China in its ideological competition. Post scraping of the defence treaty, US passed "Taiwan Relations Act" which helped to preserve autonomy for democracy to flourish in Taiwan. However, due to US policy of strategic ambiguity, the policy made clear that any military assistance could not be provided.

Secondly, the democratisation process somehow left Taiwan away from the track of its principle that both Mainland China and Taiwan are one country. This notion made drastic changes to dynamics of security dilemma concerns for the US in Taiwan Strait leading to entrapment of America in potential war situation. Forthcoming Taiwan leaders were mediating more towards establishing a separate international identity, thus amending goal to independence rather than unification. Lee's announcement of his 'two states theory' further racked up tensions in the Taiwan Strait.

The writer has made pertinent remarks about the Taiwan's journey towards achieving the goal of independent sovereign nation. Furthermore, he had cited the example of Chen Shui-bian as Taiwanese president back in 2000 and his strategic ambitions of democratisation. As the shift towards ROC being a separate entity became prominent, the US' commitment to Taiwan was questioned since Washington had no interests in fighting a war. To assess whether US should intervene in Taiwan Strait case, we need an assessment of what if Taiwan held by PRC means for US to find whether it is worth fighting for.

China has made clear that US will face stiff military conflict if it lends its military assistance towards Taiwan, which puts the democratic giant's commitment towards ROC deliberately ambiguous. US policymakers have adopted strategic ambiguity to caution Taipei leaving them to take their decisions on independence while counting on Washington support should China attack. Meanwhile, US' hidden medium of intervention in the Cross-Strait conflict has made Chinese government puzzled about how coercive Washington would be in their dealings with Taiwan. In terms of economy, Taiwan is Beijing's fifth largest trading partner.

Occupying Taiwan would direct access for top-notch semiconductor industries to PRC. Meanwhile, US' economic statistics show that Taiwan is their 10th largest trading partner which accounts for $85 billion, a paltry sum when compared with China which stands at $635 billion. So, US intervention in Cross-Strait conflict solely for economy would be devastative. Taiwan as an island also is not significant for US to project its military might.

This puts US policymakers to think twice before openly intervening in the Taiwan Strait case. The policy of strategic ambiguity, although is a safe gameplay for US, it is still dangerous which can lead to outcome of war between Taiwan and China. The writer coins that the US not openly announcing their diplomacy in Cross-Strait conflict is a gambit's gameplay. I agree with the writer regarding the arguments he made on alternatives to strategic ambiguity. Best alternative US could employ is, preserving Taiwan's democratic autonomy while keeping its bilateral relations with China straightforward, that is Washington would intervene only if China attempted to coerce reunification.

Further the author has made remarks proving the hurdles faced by the US policymakers in adopting a clear conditional commitment to Taiwan's security. Firstly, it is difficult for US to convince leaders of China and Taiwan that US has strong interests for intervention. Secondly, conditional commitments by the US does not address Taiwan's China agenda. Given the current situation, alternatives to a strategic ambiguity have daunting effect on Cross-Strait relations. In his concluding remarks, author has stated that US should wisely move in times of China dealing with its own dilemma with Taiwan. US should understand that not every interest is vital to their national security. I agree with writer's remarks stating that while ambiguity is not necessarily the best choice for US to act in Cross-Strait relations, it is certainly at the given moment. Increasing tensions has unfold several dilemmas for US to deal with while Beijing and Taipei would come to different conclusions about the degree of US intervention.

Though US necessarily does not see Taiwan as a vital economic partner, the policymakers should incorporate higher trade rates with Taiwan as it would likely neutralise increasing economic interdependencies across ROC Strait including ambiguity's biggest pitfalls. Instead of becoming obsolete in an age of increasing tensions between China and Taiwan, the US would potentially use strategic ambiguity to push themselves higher.

References & Endnotes

1. Scott L. Kastner (2006) Ambiguity, Economic Interdependence, and the US Strategic Dilemma in the Taiwan Strait, Journal of Contemporary China, 15:49, 651-669, DOI: 10.1080/10670560600836705
2. "American foreign policy. 1950-1955; basic documents. ... v.1." HathiTrust Digital Library, hdl.handle.net/2027/mdp.39015017671572. Accessed 19 Apr. 2022.

3. "Non-Aligned Movement (NAM)" 16 Apr. 2022, www.drishtiias.com/to-the-points/Paper2/non-aligned-movement-nam. Accessed 19 Apr. 2022.

4. "Taiwan Relations Act (Public Law 96-8, 22 U.S.C. 3301 et seq.)" American Institute in Taiwan, www.ait.org.tw/our-relationship/policy-history/key-u-s-foreign-policy-documents-region/taiwan-relations-act/. Accessed 19 Apr. 2022.

5. www.roc-taiwan.org/sk_en/post/2331.html. Accessed 19 Apr. 2022.

About The Author

Anirudh Phadke holds a Master of Science (Strategic Studies) from S. Rajaratnam School of International Studies (RSIS) at Nanyang Technological University (NTU), Singapore. He completed his Bachelor of Arts in Defence and Strategic Studies from Guru Nanak College (Autonomous), Chennai. He also holds a certificate in Terrorism Studies from RSIS, NTU. He founded the strategic and defence research publication called 'The Viyug'. He can be contacted via email- anirudh.r.phadke@viyug.com

Anirudh (on right side) during his post-graduate ceremony at NTU.

Follow the author on Twitter handle- @Anirudh_Phadke to receive latest updates on his publications.

Books By The Author

Research Papers on Defence and Strategic Studies Vol. 2- Terrorism, Intelligence and Cyber Warfare

About the Book

Research Papers on Defence and Strategic Studies Vol. 2 is the finest collection of research papers, Op-Eds, creative reports, critical analysis and many more on the subject matter pertaining to terrorism, intelligence and cyber warfare. The 2nd volume containts 4 chapters namely Intelligence in Peace & War, Terrorism, Intelligence, & Homeland Security, Countering Religiously-Motivated Terrorism in Southeast Asia- Issues & Challenges, and finally Conflicts in the Digital Age: Information Operations and Cyber Warfare. The book is futher divided into several sub-chapters containing the essays and other contents. The book is available (e-books, paperback, & hardback) to read and purchase from (Amazon) Kindle, Apple Books, Notion Press (for readers based in India) and other major online book distributors.

Available in E-book, Paperback & Hardback

India-China Ladakh Standoff

About the Book

From the period of the British Raj, the border issues between both the present Asian big powers existed. The Simla Convention put forth by Henry McMohan failed to formulate a definitive border between India, China, and Tibet. It ultimately leads to the Chinese annexation of Tibet. Thus from the year, 1950 the Chinese started executing massive Salami Slicing strategy to achieve their cartographic expansion goals. In the present-day scenario, the border has become a trump card for the Chinese to gain an upper hand against India whenever it tries to achieve an objective that has India's national interest merged in it. This paper analyses the current Ladakh Standoff including the Galwan Valley face off that occurred during the de-escalation process on 15th June 2020. Both the Indian and Chinese perspective are argued with proper facts and figures.

Available in E-book, Paperback & Hardback

The Viyug

The Viyug is a strategic and defence research publication launched in 2020 as an experiment during COVID-19 Pandemic (lockdown). Started as an personal blog by its founder, now it has emerged as an online and print media publication for producing top-notch and cutting edge analysis, articles, research/academic papers, and commentaries on subject matter related to defence, foreign policy, geopolitics, international affairs, public policy, and strategic signifiance with special focus on Asia-Pacific region. For business and other queries, please reach to us via email at editor@viyug.com

Website: www.viyug.com

Explore our books and Issue Brief

The Viyug Strategic Digest #1

Available in E-book, Paperback, & Hardback

About the Book

The Viyug Strategic Digest Series is a flagship digest of The Viyug published annually between the month of September to December. It is the compilation of the best articles and research papers produced by our publication during that year including the exclusive print only feature. This first issue features 5+ writers (including founder and another writer from Afghanistan) providing briefing and enlighten the readers on various topics such as Military, Strategic Studies, Public/Foreign Policy, COVID-19, and India's National Security.

Issue Breif

Jus ad Bellum and Global Terrorism

About the Book

Global terrorism poses a challenge to the relevancy and application of the principles of Just War. Jus ad bellum has come into disfavor and disuse. However, policymakers have generally dismissed jus ad bellum principles without a serious policy or legal debate. Jus ad bellum principles remain relevant to the modern era and the war on global terrorism. A proper application of the principles is required to obtain the proper legal and policy guidance. The Viyug's Issue Brief #2 deals on Jus ad Bellum and its relevance in 21st century and modern warfare including cyber terrorism, aerial warfare etc. A finest brief for a reform of American foreign policy and on the use of force.

Writer: Johnny B. Davis (International Law Attorney, Professor at the Liberty University Helms School of Government and also an Army National Guard at JAG).

Podcasts by The Viyug

Podcasts and audiobooks produced by us are available on across all major online platforms like Spotify, Apple Podcasts, and more.

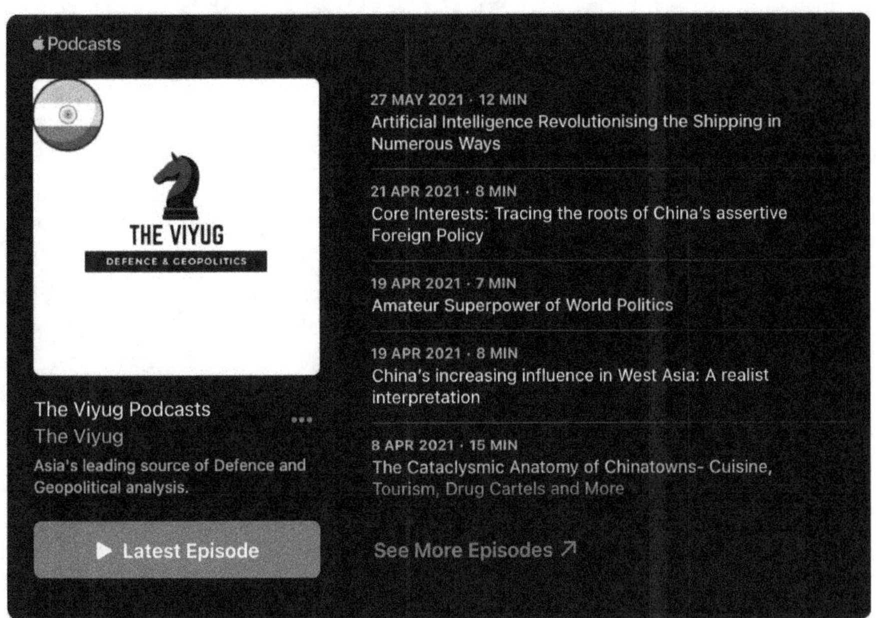

The Viyug on Apple Podcasts

The Viyug's Podcasts on Spotify

Follow the Twitter handle- @the_viyug for latest updates on articles and publications.

Publish with Us

If you are a writer/researcher on subject matter of our interests then publish your commentaries, research papers, reports, issue brief, & books with The Viyug and kickstart your career today. for more visit us at website- www.viyug.com

9 798888 491225